"... short but meaty chapters on the peace and joy of contemplation open to all—religious and lay ... in simple, clear and realistic language ... This book should be on the shelf of everyone striving for peace and serenity. It is a must!"—*Review for Religious*

"Pennington ... while seeing membership in the monastic community as a special vocation, nevertheless sees monastic prayer and practice simply as an intensified form of the life to which all Christians are called."—*National Catholic Reporter*

"Is there a separate spirituality for those living 'in the world' and those cloistered? Should there be? Can the two be grafted together without adversely affecting or distorting the integrity of either? ... This book comes as Basil Pennington's answer to these questions—ones that have been put to him time after time by earnest seekers ... Fasting, work, obedience, liturgy, silence and solitude, among other topics, are treated tenderly and with understanding ... a valuable addition to the literature promoting a deeper Christian life, and should be thoughtfully and prayerfully read and used."—*Spiritual Life*

"For all who are seeking ways to 'grow in grace and in the knowledge of our Lord and Savior Jesus Christ' Father Pennington offers very literate guidelines and persuasive counsel in A PLACE APART ... In positive and encouraging terms [he] discusses various aspects of monastic life—silence, fasting, obedi- 'ence, work ... friendship, joy. And he does so not in a way to make those 'in the world' envy or marvel but in a way to help them improve their own spiritual life, their own Christian commitment."—*Columbia*

"[Pennington's] advice should appeal even to those committed to active work for peace and justice ... Father Basil communicates in a warm, human way. Most everyone would be touched."—*Spiritual Book News*

M. Basil Pennington, O.C.S.O.

A PLACE APART

Monastic Prayer and Practice

for Everyone

IMAGE BOOKS
A DIVISION OF DOUBLEDAY & COMPANY, INC.
GARDEN CITY, NEW YORK
1985

Image Books edition published March 1985 by special arrangement with
Doubleday & Company, Inc.

Library of Congress Cataloging in Publication Data

Pennington, M. Basil.
A place apart.

1. Spiritual life—Catholic authors.   I. Title.
BX2350.2.P433   1983   248.4'82
ISBN: 0-385-19706-3
Library of Congress Catalog Card Number: 81–43566

Biblical quotations are from The Jerusalem Bible.

Contents

Foreword

I first visited Saint Joseph's Abbey several years ago as I was preparing for a course in the theology of prayer. I was to take this course in the fall as an elective in a graduate program in psychiatric-mental health nursing at the Catholic University of America. It was a beautiful August day as I ventured onto the grounds of the Trappist monastery. I sheepishly knocked on the door of the guest house and was graciously welcomed by Brother Jude, a young, bearded monk who radiated joy, happiness, and peace. I told Brother of my reasons for visiting the monastery—I wanted to get some information about Centering Prayer, a "new" form of prayer I had heard about. I wanted to know if there was some reading material I could get or someone I could talk with about this method of prayer. Brother Jude asked me if I would like to speak with Father Basil Pennington. This was the name I had heard associated with Centering Prayer, so I was delighted at the prospect of meeting this man. Within a few minutes a tall, bearded monk entered the parlor where I was waiting. At that moment I embarked upon a new path on my spiritual pilgrimage—a path that has been rich and fulfilling; a path of happiness, joy, and peace; a path filled with challenges and supports required to meet those challenges.

For those who have not met, or do not know of, Father Basil, he is a monk of Saint Joseph's Abbey at Spencer, Massachusetts. He has been a monk for thirty-one years and is regarded by many as one of the great spiritual masters and one of the great spiritual authors of our time. His books *Daily We Touch Him* and *Centering Prayer* are already spiritual classics. His published journals have shared much of his thoughts and insights during some of the significant times of his spiritual pilgrimage.

This present book comes largely out of the experience of Father Basil during the four years that he was vocation father at Saint Joseph's Abbey. During those years hundreds of young men spent time in a small stone lodging on the monastery grounds referred to as The Cottage. These people were exploring whether or not they were being called to a monastic vocation and, if so, where they were being called to serve. I was one of the hundreds who had the tremendous, grace-filled privilege of participating in what has come to be called The Cottage Talks. In the evening, between Vespers and Compline, the men staying in The Cottage would meet with Father Basil and discuss some value, tradition, or practice inherent in the monastic life, how it was lived in the daily life of a monk, and how we might incorporate it in our daily lives as laymen. At the urging of people such as myself, Father Basil consented to write this book, which would make the content of those Cottage Talks available for all spiritual pilgrims.

My journey has been greatly enriched as a result of my

exposure to Father Basil. I am very excited about this book and the opportunity it will provide for all to experience, in a somewhat different format but experience nonetheless, Father Basil, The Cottage Talks, and, through them, monastic values, traditions, and practices.

As I reflect on the contents of this very significant addition to the resources on spirituality available to the lay person, I am amazed at the wide audience to which A *Place Apart* appeals. I am sure the hundreds of men who passed through The Cottage will welcome this comprehensive resource containing what they may have experienced only in part. Anyone serious about seeking God will find Father Basil's words extremely valuable, but especially those who are influenced by or are attracted to Benedictine-Cistercian spirituality. Those who have not yet been exposed to Benedictine-Cistercian spirituality will find herein a definitive resource flowing out of the experience of a man who has for over three decades studied, experienced, and lived Benedictine-Cistercian spirituality and who has sought to make available to others what has been passed on from one generation of monks to another for hundreds of years. This book will also be very useful to Christian discussion groups, adult Christian education coordinators, religion teachers, theology instructors, CCD instructors, and directors of formation and renewal in religious communities. It will be of value to spiritual mothers and fathers as a resource to them in their role as spiritual guides.

I welcome it as a mental health professional who approaches the client or patient from a holistic-theoretical framework. This will be an excellent resource for people such as myself in efforts to help clients or patients to better meet their spiritual needs. Holistically oriented health care providers have many resources available to them to give them direction in their interventions to help their clients or patients with biological, psychological, and sociological needs. This book will provide us with an excellent resource for our work with clients or patients who want to focus on their spiritual needs as well.

Finally, what follows will be of value to those concerned about political and social issues. Its focus is on a comprehensive model through which peace can be achieved for us all as we work together as a human family to respond to the needs of all people and pray together with serious personal and corporate commitment: "Thy Kingdom come!"

Father Basil's definition of happiness is this: it is knowing what we want and knowing either that we have it or we are on our way to getting it. The way he clearly describes a goal may help those who have not clearly formalized a goal for themselves. With a clearly defined target, decisions become easier; we focus our attention and decide if what we are considering will bring us closer to our desire or impede our progress. Father Basil's book clearly defines a goal: a life of love, joy, and peace. This book also provides a clear and detailed map which will help us stay on course and arrive safely at our destination.

If we are dissatisfied in any way with our thoughts, feelings, and/or behavior the most effective way of reversing that situation is to expand our perceptual field in the area of our philosophical and spiritual beliefs. Our thoughts flow from these values and our feelings flow out of our thoughts. Finally our behavior or deeds and actions flow out of all three but especially out of our feelings. Father

Basil's book is valuable because it influences in a positive, healthy, and theologically sound way our philosophical and spiritual beliefs. As we read and begin to incorporate the contents of this book in our lives we will see our thoughts, feelings, and behavior change. We will experience ourselves become more like our Master in thought, word, and deed.

A *Place Apart* should help us in our efforts to become more committed Christians who are ever deepening in our love for God, our fellows, and our world. It should assist us in our joy-filled commitment to work for the coming of the Kingdom. This book should help us in our efforts to transform a troubled world, that at times appears to be on a self-destructive course, into a world of love, peace, and joy.

For the book to work in this way, I think the reader needs to take each chapter very seriously. This is what I did. I very comprehensively assessed where I was with respect to each value, tradition, and practice; how I got there and where I wanted to be. I established for myself short and long range goals and designed a plan to move in the direction of incorporating into my life more fully each value, tradition, and practice. Then I began to implement the plan and decided to systematically evaluate my progress on a monthly basis during my monthly day of recollection. You may want to evaluate your progress at a different interval such as every week, every quarter, or every year. Whatever interval you decide will work best for you, decide on a way to remind yourself of your desire to evaluate your progress regularly and systematically; an entry on your calendar might serve as a sure reminder.

You might want to work on the incorporation into your

life of these values, traditions, and practices with a supportive person such as a spiritual mother, father or friend. Some might find a group that meets regularly as a valuable support system where members of the group work together on growing as ever more committed Christians. During these group sessions the individual members can share their challenges, setbacks, and successes and receive love and support from one another.

I thank Father Basil for the privilege of writing this foreword and for the opportunity to share these thoughts with you, the reader. I am grateful that we have this resource for our spiritual journey made available to us by one of the spiritual masters of our time. I want to close in thanking all the monks of Spencer Abbey for their part in this book for it really comes out of the experience of the entire Spencer community with Father Basil serving as the spokesman for the vision of the entire community of that great spiritual center. On behalf of the laity that have been so enriched by Father Basil's books I thank the community for the support and encouragement it has provided to Father Basil to follow the inspiration of the Holy Spirit to share its rich spiritual insights, values, traditions, and practices with a hungry and thirsting world. May we all be encouraged and nourished by the prayers of the Spencer community as we seek the Lord where our Creator has placed us and where he challenges us to call forth all of creation to utter in one accord a great, sincere, and total "Yes" to our God.

Michael Moran, USN

Introduction

I received a letter last week from a tried and concerned father: "My son Joe is struggling, too. After he finishes school he would like to enter a monastery for two or three years to sort things out." Joe probably was aware that his desire was not unique, but I suspect he might be surprised by how widespread it is. He and his contemporaries would be even more surprised by the fact that they are aspiring to step into an age-old tradition of other cultures. In some Buddhist countries it has been the expected thing that every young man from crown prince to peasant will spend some time in the monastic habit. In the Hindu tradition a young man will sit for some years at the feet of a guru as a student of life, then he will go out and become a householder. After his children are raised and grandchildren begin to put in their appearance, he may again embrace the life of a renunciant and even return to the forest as a sadhu.

In a world where the human person's most basic aspirations for peace, justice, and joy seem to be hopelessly thwarted, where hope is indeed hope against hope, where a game called deterrence, a global Russian roulette, gambles with the lives of every woman, man, and child in the human family, more and more men and women look for the "peace the world cannot give," look for the kingdom which is to come, the kingdom of peace that is already within us: "The Kingdom of God is within you." They see the motto carved over the portals of monasteries: PAX INTRANTIBUS—Peace to those who enter. They want that peace. They rightly sense that this first gift of the Risen Lord belongs by right to all for whom Christ died and rose. The monastic heritage, the heritage from the Church of Jerusalem even though it became the church of the desert, remains the essential heritage of the Christian community. "My kingdom is not of this world." Even while they dwell in the cities of the world and take their active and responsible part in the political and social ordering of this world Christians know they belong more radically to another society and it is from that society they can draw their strength and peace to minister to the world till it be transformed. The monastery, the monastic way of life, sacramentalizes and incarnates, gives witness to and makes present—or should—the kingdom of peace and justice and love. Christian pilgrims on mission to the world—"Go forth to all nations . . ."—want to keep in touch with their true destiny, to live as far as possible the rich life of their own kingdom. We might say then, if it will not be misunderstood, that they want to keep in touch with the monastic dimension of their lives and to enjoy the fruit that comes from cultivating that.

Saint Peter has written to the Christian community, to you and to me:

> Look for the coming of the day of God and try to has-
> ten it! Because of it, the heavens will be destroyed in
> flames and the elements will melt away in a blaze.
> What we await are new heavens and a new earth
> where, according to his promise, the justice of God
> will reside.

I do not know if this means that there must be a nuclear
holocaust, that as God once cleansed the earth by water to
give the human family a new start, he will again cleanse
the earth, this time by fire, to bring to an end the rampant
social injustice that desecrates his creation and open the
way to his kingdom of justice. It does mean, though, that
we need not fear even a nuclear holocaust. For our God
has everything in his hands and even out of such a massive
evil he can and will bring good. It is a call for us, his people, to ardently seek the establishment of his kingdom:
Thy Kingdom come. But how?

Peter goes on:

> So, beloved, while waiting for this, make every effort
> to be found without stain or defilement and at peace
> in his sight. Consider that our Lord's patience is
> directed toward salvation.

What we can do now to bring about his kingdom of justice is to cooperate in the establishment of justice in that
portion of his kingdom over which we have some immediate control: ourselves. Let us begin the pursuit of justice
and peace by cleaning up our own lives and establishing
peace within our own hearts. In the face of all the chaos,
disorder, and violence that rage around us there is hope of
establishing peace within if we can enter into the mind of

the Lord, adopt his attitude of patience with the blindly sinful, and have confidence that his patient permissiveness is indeed directed toward the salvation of all, even if we cannot comprehend how this may be so: "My ways are not your ways, nor my thoughts your thoughts, says the Lord; but as high as the heavens are above the earth so are my ways beyond your ways and my thoughts beyond your thoughts." So let us have confidence in him and his ways.

> You are forewarned, beloved brothers, be on your guard lest you be led astray by the errors of the wicked, and forfeit the security you enjoy.

There is indeed the danger that we will succumb, as have so many in imitation of and competition with atheistic materialists, and embrace the idolatry of technology, placing our hope in armaments and thus lose the inner peace that should be ours in the knowledge that we are securely held in the infinitely powerful and caring love of our Lord.

> Rather grow in grace and in the knowledge of our Lord and Savior Jesus Christ.

Here is the true source of peace and security. As grace frees us from the bondage of our sins and fears, the true knowledge of our Savior and his powerful love will be able to take hold in us; and through us, in our homes, our communities, our nations, and our world. The whole will be leavened. As Saint Paul wrote to us: "God's folly is wiser than men's, and his weakness more powerful than men's."

When we live out of the faith and hope that is ours as Christians then, as our Master said, we are salt to salt the earth and preserve it; we are light to enlighten the world. If the monastery is as it were "a city set on a hill," it is there not only to "be seen by men so that they may praise the heavenly Father," but also to encourage each and every Christian to light his or her own lamp and "set it on a stand where it gives light to all in the house." If Christians are invited to cultivate the monastic dimension of their lives it is not just for their own peace and joy, their own fulfillment. We are one Body, one human family. We are called to perfection so that we may be perfect as our heavenly Father, a beneficent source for good and bad alike.

In this volume I have sought to share some of the values and practices of the monastic life and suggest ways in which those in the world, single or married, young or old, might incorporate them into their lives and the life of their households or communities. These chapters come basically out of colloquia or monastic bull sessions which took place each evening around the large fireplace in "The Cottage." The Cottage is a small stone bungalow which stands within the monastic enclosure at Saint Joseph's Abbey. It was the home of the man who owned the property before the monks came. He had built it himself and gave it a very special warmth and charm. The whole house seems to center around the great hearth. For some years we have used it to house men who were interested in getting a closer look at monastic life as part of a discernment process to determine their vocation. Each evening after supper in the interval between Vespers and Compline, I would meet with these men around the hearth and we would explore in turn different monastic values, not only as they existed in the tradition and as we monks live them today, but as they might become a part of these men's lives in the world. The vast majority of the men who joined in these colloquia will never become monks. I welcomed over three hundred a year in The Cottage but only eight or ten into the community. But it is my earnest prayer that each man who shared in these colloquia will have taken away from them some practical insights which will motivate and enrich his life no matter what path he is following. The publication of the fruit of these colloquia I hope will support that.

The decision, though, to try to bring together some of the rich content of those sharings for publication did not arise immediately from that hope. It has arisen rather from a desire to respond to the request of many men and women, not a few of whom I have first come into contact with through the sharing of our prayer tradition in the Centering Prayer. Having experienced a real enrichment from incorporating this one aspect—certainly a very central aspect—of monastic life into their busy active lives in the world, they have asked for assistance in exploring the possibility of incorporating other traditional monastic values. As a contemplative monk, I did not want to launch into another program of workshops, yet I saw and felt deeply the validity and significance of the request. This volume seeks to make some response to it. I pray that the Holy Spirit dwelling in you will complete it and make up for the insufficiency of what is offered here.

I have to thank many for the reality of this volume: the abbots who have initiated me into the monastic life and guided me, the wonderful community of monks who have been the constant supportive context of my living it, the many inquirers who sat around the fireplace in The Cottage and called forth these sharings, Father Win Lewis and Commander Mike Moran, who helped me finally get them on paper—I am especially indebted to Mike for his gracious and valuable Foreword—and the wonderful sister who turned my scratch into a readable typescript. I feel confident their prayer and love will empower these pages to be fruitful in your life. I am grateful to you, too, the reader, for allowing me to share in this way with you. May the Lord of Love, to whom above all we owe all, bring us all together to eternal life. Then my joy will be complete.

Fr. M. Basil

June 18, 1982 *Monk of Spencer*

I write this on the anniversary of my entrance into the monastic life very conscious that it has been a gift given to me for the whole Church and the entire human family. It is good to be able to share it.

A Place Apart

A Place Apart

At one point, as the French railway train moves toward
Grenoble, knowledgeable travelers can be seen looking in-
tently out the north windows and then excitedly poking
their neighbors. They have spotted it, high up on the rug-
ged slope, the virtually inaccessible sanctuary of La Grande
Chartreuse, the epitome of all that is monastic. I have
never ascended to that fabled charterhouse, but seeing it
brought back memories of my first monastic visit in
Europe. As our ship eased into the Barcelona harbor, the
radar picked out the mammoth granite stylites that jut
out from the plains of northern Spain just west of the city.
It took our car hours to wind around and around as we
gradually ascended to the large historic Benedictine abbey
that is nestled in the uppermost reaches of the Montserrat.
As we walked along the embankment in front of the monastery, looking down on the port far below, we suddenly
found ourselves literally in the clouds, as a low bank
moved in upon us.

Monks reach for the heights. They also seek their

apartness in other ways. Sergius Bolshakoff describes his visit to Uusi Valamo in 1954:

> Our small boat nosed its way through the bewildering succession of lakes of northern Saimaa. The farther we moved to the northeast, the wilder and emptier the country became. Tall and silent forests lined the shores of the lakes through which we were passing. Hardly any dwellings or fields were to be seen. The region is all forest, bathed in silence and solitude.

But one does not have to go to the heights or the depths to find a place apart. Anyone who has penetrated an inner-city Carmel with its high walls, its grilles, and its curtains, knows how much even in the midst of a teeming city a monastic community can set itself apart and create a climate of apartness.

That is the important thing, the sense of apartness. The heavenly voice said to Arsenius, the praying courtier, "Flee, be silent, pray." And the palace favorite made his first step toward becoming the desert father. If one note is to characterize the true monk, it is this: he is the one who has gone apart, to be in some way alone—*monos*, alone, one with God. Gone apart to find silence to pray, to commune with God.

The follower of Christ, the Christian who wants to follow Christ, to live the Christian life to the full, not so much extensively in activities as intensively in act, remembers how often his Master went apart to pray. His years of growth were so hidden, we know virtually nothing of them. After he received his commission to ministry through a voice from heaven: "Listen to him," he disappears into the desert for weeks of solitude and silence, and, we may be sure, prayer. As his busy years of healing ministry unfolded, again and again, alone or with his chosen ones, he went apart:

> When Jesus received this news [of John's beheading] he withdrew by boat to a lonely place where they could be by themselves. (Matt. 14:13)

> After sending the crowds away he went up into the hills by himself to pray. (Matt. 14:23)

> Six days later, Jesus took with him Peter and James and his brother John and led them up a high mountain where they could be alone. (Matt. 17:1)

> Jesus was going up to Jerusalem, and on the way he took the Twelve apart to speak with them. (Matt. 20:17)

> The apostles rejoined Jesus and told him all they had done and taught. Then he said to them, "You must come away to some lonely place all by yourselves and rest for a while." (Mark 6:30)

The monk goes apart in imitation of his Master and primarily for the same purpose as his Master: to be one with him in communion with the Father. The monk seeks to be alone—all one—at oneness with all, in that oneness we find in God. He has had some intimation of the reality of baptism, that he has been made one with the Son. His whole movement is to the Father in the Son through the Holy Spirit, conscious that in Christ he is one with all, that his movement with Christ's has a universal mediatory role.

"The fascination of trifles obscures the good," says the Wise Man. It is difficult in the midst of much doing and seeing to keep alive and present to the deepest reality, to the really real. And so the monk goes apart to find a greater quietness, a daily sameness, a stability that forestalls some of the onrush of new sights and sounds. He can, of course, bring distracting things with him into his solitude. The ultimate folly: to bring the whole world with him through television. He will, of course, bring much with him—all he has ever experienced—in his memory. And the interior television will give him lots of replay. He will have to learn to turn off that inner dialogue, or better, to sink to the deeper places where its frequency is unattuned; or best, to integrate it into the growing harmony that allows all to speak of God and to God in him.

His solitude, his apartness, first allows him to gain that perspective on himself and then on the rest of creation that leads to such an integration. Isaac of Stella, speaking of the Master's going up on to a mountain, comments: "My Lord Jesus, and perhaps he alone, can in a crowd not be distracted by the crowd from seeing the crowd." But it is only the person "who sees the crowd well, who can fully turn from its attractions, easily go out from it and freely forget it."

Distance is needed for perspective and true spiritual freedom. But the solitude we most seek and for which this physical and inner solitude are a preparation is the solitude to be found in God. Of this solitude, Saint Bernard exclaimed: "O blessed solitude, my sole beatitude!" Of this solitude I really cannot write. It is to be experienced. It is so solitary, there is nothing of which to write. Yet, in this

solitude, all is. And one knows in this solitude that he has
in the power of God, in the Christness of his person, the
love power, the being to lift up the whole of creation. And,
in fact, in his very being there he is lifting up the whole
creation, every woman, man, and child, and all else, animate and inanimate. In his solitary kiss of the divine, in
entering into the embrace of God, he brings all forward, a
stride closer to that fullness and consummation that comes
about from the creation's receiving in fullest freedom the
fullness of the embrace of Divine Creating Love.

The call to solitude, to know and enjoy a certain
amount of physical solitude, and certainly, to enter into
the solitude of God, is not the exclusive prerogative of the
monk (even though it might be the essential characteristic
of his particular vocation). When I think of the role of
solitude in the life of the active lay person, the name
(though there are many) that most immediately and prominently comes to the fore in my mind is that of the great
Father of India, Mahatma Gandhi. Father, grandfather,
lawyer, statesman, activist, pacifist, his life could not have
been fuller, and yet, or because of this, it was a life that always found time for solitude. Even when the whole of the
subcontinent awaited his every word and the future of his
people and his nation hung upon him, or because of this,
each week Gandhi faithfully took a day apart and entered
into silence and solitude. (In the light of such an example,
what person can dare say they cannot afford to take time
for apartness—indeed, who can afford *not* to take time for
apartness?)

Gandhi was a man of such power because he was
sourced. He was a man of such clarity and perspective be-

cause he regularly went apart. He accomplished so much for his people and was such a realized and complete person himself because he acted first for God.

> I can testify that I may live without air and water, but not without Him (God). You may pluck out my eye, but that cannot kill me. You may chop off my nose, but that cannot kill me. You blast my belief in God and then I am dead.

Certainly we are not all called to be another Gandhi. But we all do want to be powerful—powerful in ways of life and love, calling others forth to fuller life and love. We all do want to be fulfilled and realized persons, living according to our own fullness, finding therein the joy, the peace, the happiness for which God has made us. To do this, to keep perspective, to be sourced, to be in harmony with who we truly are, we have to go apart, according to our own needs and rhythm.

We do not all have the flexibility in our lives to be able to make the time and establish the space for a weekly day of apartness. But, let's be *very* realistic here. There is in the lives of most of us a good bit more freedom and flexibility to organize such a dimension, *if we really want to*. In setting about integrating the values of apartness into our lives, this would be the first question: Do I see a real value in having regularly a time apart? At this point I hope most will answer, Yes. But for many this will still be more an intellectual conviction of variable strength than an experiential knowledge that amounts to almost a physical hunger. I recall a line from the letter of a friend speaking of this: "As for the time apart, all I can say is that when I miss it, I miss it." Well said!

Do I really want time apart? Do I know I need time apart? I do make time and place for what I want, what I need. Recently a couple proudly showed me their new home. Prominent in the tour was their prayer room. I daresay that five years earlier, if this same couple were setting up that house, that little room would probably have been a study or a guest room. But they had come to know the importance of apartness in their lives, even their daily lives, and they made a place for it.

I think to have a place is important. I speak of it even before the question of time because, making the time (note: I say "making the time"—we don't just "find" it), we have to have some place to spend it. Moreover, a constituted place stands there beckoning to us, reminding us to make the time. Probably very few will be able to use a whole room in their home exclusively as a place for apartness, for prayer and solitude. Yet, I believe, more homeowners than one might first suspect will be able to do this and will do it, once they have reconstituted their hierarchy of values and readjusted their living space accordingly. For most, the at-home place apart may well have to be an alcove, a dormer, a closet, a corner of their room or some less used room. A shrine of sorts will mark it off from the space around it, will proclaim a Presence, a place of encounter. Everyone has personal tastes and attractions. It is interesting to look into the cells (as monks call their rooms; it has nothing to do with prison cells. "Cell" comes from the Latin word *cella*, related to the word *coelum*, heaven, the place where one enjoys God) around our monastery. One, in the style of Eastern Christian homes, has a large shrine of icons opposite the entrance, a lamp ever flickering before them. In stark contrast to this, another cell is completely nude. An expansive lightsome wall speaks powerfully of divine solitude. Another boasts but an empty cross, inviting ascension, transfixion, and transformation. Most cells have the Bible enthroned, and in some this is the centering presence of the place apart. One has a rich collection of relics—the saints are there to support the solitary. To each his own. The important thing is that there is this place which, when one goes there, even if the going is no more than turning one's chair around, one has a sense of having gone apart.

If one cannot find such a niche anywhere at home—and that may very well be the case in many instances—then one has to look farther afield, perhaps a nearby church or chapel. A friend in Washington has arranged with a community of sisters a few blocks from his apartment to slip into their usually empty chapel. Most pastors are quite willing to give a church key to a sincere pray-er for off-hour use. One might find a park, a library, a museum. Thomas Merton, during a certain period in New York, found his place apart in The Cloisters museum. A businessman might create his prayer corner in his office. A car has been a hermitage for many. Each one who wants to will find his or her place near at hand for daily apartness, and will make the time to enter into that place.

Again, people will have their own rhythms. The times of sunrise and sunset, morning and evening, sacred to almost all traditions, may have difficulty fitting into the pattern of

some lives. Moderns hardly live by the sun. Electricity turns
night into day. Maybe it is a bit of our perversity that even
as tykes we want to stay up as late as we can and get up as
late as we can. At first, rather naked conviction and disci-
pline may have to carve out our time apart with a certain
amount of loving ruthlessness—both in regard to ourselves
and in regard to others. Don't be afraid to experiment with
times and rhythms. But seek to come to discern, perhaps
with the help of your spiritual guide or friend, what really
works for you. By that I mean, how much time apart you
need to keep true perspective, to be truly sourced, to experience in your life in an abiding way the fruits of the
Spirit: love, joy, peace, patience, kindness, benignity.

For some, the rhythm may not be daily, or the daily
time apart minimal. Larger spaces and other intervals will
be more important. For all, though, the daily will not be
sufficient. There will need to be periodically more
significant times apart if you are to derive the full benefit
of this value. The couple whom I mentioned above, who
have a prayer room in their home, do nonetheless seek out
a house of prayer near the abbey for a monthly time apart.
Others come to the abbey itself for their weekly or
monthly day apart. For most there is some retreat house,
monastery, or house of prayer within reach where they can
come to find a place apart for more significant sourcing.
Again, where there is determination there is fruition.
Though, in the end, if age, sickness, disability, or some
other factor prohibits, you may have just to close the door
of your room for a day or make the daily place special in
some way. Again, too, the rhythm will be according to each
one's needs and attractions. A day a month, a week a year

is common, but not all that common. Find what really works for you.

There is something of the monk in each one of us. Not to be neglected in this apartness is that precious cell in the heart. There is deep within us a place apart. Perhaps if we begin to explore it we will discover we have made it into a bit of a storeroom. Perhaps it is even so crammed with junk we can hardly get in or close the door. Saint Benedict in his Rule reminds monks: "The oratory should be what it is called—a place of prayer. Let nothing else be done or kept there." We may have to do some housecleaning. But we do have this place within where we can at any moment retire, close the door (as our Lord said) and enjoy for that moment a place apart. Get to know that inner cell. You will come to love it and it will come to be a true friend. When you are harassed or weary you will begin to experience it reaching out to you, beckoning: Come apart and rest awhile. In its deep, cool darkness, sometimes illumined by a light not of our making, a moment can be a refreshing step into eternity, a coming home to the solitude of God.

"A place apart"—there are many places apart for each one of us: those we create, those we find, those created for us. Each is a gift and has its gifts for us. Seek and you shall find. Taste and see!

Watching in the Night

Nick snuggled down a little more deeply, tucking the blankets under his chin. The bells could not be said to have disturbed his sleep. Rather they invited him to enjoy it all the more, as he sensed himself embraced by the loving prayers of the monks and found a deeper sense of security. Perhaps when he first settled here thirty years ago to find work at the abbey as a carpenter the bells spoke more of material security. But now, especially in the last year since Ann had died and he lay alone in his bed at night, the bells spoke deeply to him of another more important security. Even while the world around him slept, and he slept, he knew that he and his children and his grandchildren and all whom he loved were being embraced and raised up by the prayers of the monks in the night.

Across the fields, surely not more than three miles away, on the western slope, Adaire, too, heard the vigil bell from the abbey. She rose quickly, wrapped herself in her ankle-length terry robe, and set about stirring up the fire in the stove. Another log soon had it crackling and glowing, changing a cold dark room into a place of warmth and wel-

come. Adaire had sought out and settled into this little
cottage in sight of the abbey, and within earshot of the
bells, after having completed her twenty years as one of
New York's "finest." The nearby monastery set the rhythm
of her new life. She opened the folding door at the end of
her room. As she lit the little oil lamps, and the gilt background of each icon picked up the liveliness of the dancing
flames, Adaire found herself no longer alone. She was in
the Presence of the Pantocrator, the Maker of All, and the
Theotokos, the Holy Mother of God, and all her favorite
friends among the heavenly court. She prostrated, and her
prayer rose like incense, one with the prayer of the monks
in the abbey church, with monks and nuns everywhere,
and with all the solitary lay folk like herself who entered
into this nocturnal praise.

Farther down the hill, the bell gently intruded itself into
the slumber of John and Maria. They said nothing, but
drew more closely together and felt the beat of each
other's hearts. They needed no words at this moment
when their hearts rose together to the Throne of Mercy in
a whole bouquet of sentiments: love, gratitude, petition,
wonder, humility, and total being. Unlike Nick, who came
here to work, and Adaire, who came to retire, John and
Maria had always been here. By American standards theirs
was an old family, long farming the land. When rumor
first told of the coming of the monks they had no idea
what it might mean, but to these devout Catholics it
sounded good. Now, John would be hard put to find quite
the right words. He might more easily point to the more
obvious effects. Not only he and Maria, but the children,
too, had come to know the daily journey to the top of the

hill for early Mass. And there was a lot more prayer in the home. But it was more than that. The young ones might speak of it as the "vibes." Yes, the "vibes" had changed. There was a new peace upon the land, and it seemed more fruitful, too—at least to this experienced farmer. Something more than the sound of bells flowed out from the abbey on the hill.

On the crest of the hill, gleaming in the moonlight, the fieldstone abbey looked as if it had always been there—something that had naturally pushed itself up out of the soil, as indeed each of the stones had, before they were collected by the monks and brought together to create a twelfth-century abbey in twentieth-century New England. Inside its long, narrow church, the guest retreatants in the front and the hopeful candidates in the rear heard the bell, accompanied by the rustling of robes as the monks filled the stalls and then, standing as it were at attention, raised their voices:

> O Lord, open my lips,
> And my tongue shall declare your praise.

"Come, let us adore," sang the cantor. And the retreatants joined the monks in adoring, praising, and thanking, the unspoken petitions in their hearts laid bare before their Father, not to be denied. The imagination of the candidates easily clothed them in the white cowl, set them in one of the stalls, repeating with all the choir: Yes, come, let us adore!

In some reflective moments the monks were not unaware that the "vibes" of their prayer flowed out from the abbey not only into the immediate environs, but encircling the whole globe in a current of peace and caring love, uniting with the prayer of all and lifting up each one. But in the midst of the prayerful chant they were more conscious of the ascent to God, or rather of God Himself, than of all that ascended with their prayer and flowed out from it. If challenged by questioning as to what they were about, they would not first think or speak of the empowering and uplifting, though they certainly would not deny it. While they may not be comfortable with too gross a presentation of the "powerhouse" analogy, the intercessory role of the monk is a commonplace. And monks realize well that when the consciousness of one person is raised, the whole of humanity is raised; when the quality of life of one improves, all improve. Or, to put it in another, more biblical, way, the increased health and vitality of any one cell vitalizes the whole Body of Christ.

But the monk might think more readily of his Master and see his rising in the night for prayer as an imitation, a following of him. At the significant moments of his life, Jesus entered into a watch of prayer. As he inaugurated his healing ministry at Capernaum—

> In the morning, long before dawn, he got up and left the house, and went off to a lonely place and prayed there. (Mark 1:35)

When it came time to choose his apostles—

> He went out into the hills to pray; and he spent the whole night in prayer to God. (Luke 6:12)

The monk prays in the night in imitation of his Lord and Master but also because it expresses the very essence of his life. When Saint Benedict came to spell out the signs which are to guide the novice master in discerning a true monastic vocation, he set forth as the first and absolutely fundamental one: Does he truly seek God? If we listen to what is deepest in us we find a deep longing for God; a mind that seeks all Truth; a desire to know that will be satisfied only when it finds the ultimate Answer that ties everything together. And more important, more urgent, and in the end more profoundly at the center of our being, there is a heart that longs for a limitless love, a heart that seeks that Love who is God Himself—the only Love big enough to fill all our void. Indeed, if we listen attentively we hear this seeking deep in every human voice, see it in every human eye that opens itself to us; we perceive it in all the restless strivings of our brothers and sisters. And in the rest of the creation—the whole creation is in travail, groaning, seeking its fulfillment in the fullness of the redemption that is to come to it.

One of the awesome models for monks is the great Arsenius. We are told that as the sun set he raised his arms in prayer and did not lower them until the rising sun cast its shadows on the ground before him, when he prostrated before the Risen Son. Not many can approximate this holy monk's steadfastness. Even Moses had to be supported by Aaron and Hur as he watched through a day of battle. True, Christian monks in the Byzantine tradition do still watch through the night before Sundays and feasts. But Saint Benedict legislated for a weaker lot. He rouses his monks from their beds at the seventh hour of the night (around 2 or 3 A.M.) after they are rested. But what else can one do at that hour of the night and in the subsequent hours but watch and wait for the dawn? It is a time of seeking.

It may be that something deep within twists and stretches, taut with longing and expectation. Or the soul may lie as quiet as a dewdrop on the grass on Saint Joseph's Hill, crystallizing as it gathers in the light of the aurora until the first glint of the rising sun turns it into a fiery diamond to be laid in homage at the feet of the Risen Son.

On rarer occasions, the monk's watching is the bride's eager straining to catch a glimpse through the lattice of faith or the bridal party's excited listening for the footfall at the door. But even bridesmaids have been known to fall asleep in their watching. There will be those dull nights, when perhaps a damp chill will lie heavy, like fog, on the spirit, and the thought of the great Arsenius will mock the flagging monk. If he is watching in his cell his eyes will cast furtive glances toward the inviting mattress in the corner. He may have to flee to the outdoors to let the rudeness of the night arouse him, or else strain his weary muscles, rising and falling in prostrations until the heart pounds again to supply the holy exertions and irrigate the sluggish brain. More often it seems to be a lot of muddled reverie before the Lord, a quiet being-with a Loved One, a deep sense that this is right, that this is satisfying to some deep emptiness within. He is coming—it is good to be watching and waiting.

This experiential sense of watching and of the goodness of it usually does not come at once. The novice may be fortunate enough to have a period of honeymoon excitement when the watch is all sweetness and consolation. Or he may not. Soon enough it is fidelity to a practice, an observance, that carries the watcher on. But it is a fidelity that is in time rewarded. Maybe at first only sporadically, but in time it becomes a state of soul, something precious, not all that easy to describe, but precious and prized. It is a restive resting that has its painful delight. It is a time of love, a love more anticipated than experienced, perhaps, but a time of love—a very real "living with" an apparently absent and longed-for Lover. These hours of watching come to be among the most prized hours of the monk's day.

But to be practical, most "monks in the world" can hardly hope to adjust the clocks of their lives so as to be able to rise at the "seventh hour" of the night to enjoy a predawn watch. At best, with careful planning and the sure knowledge that there will be days when it just won't work out, one can plan to retire early enough to have a reasonable period to "watch" before beginning his or her more formal morning prayer. It might be set off with lighting a candle or a bit of incense, a prostration before a holy image, or the enthroned Scriptures, a reading from the Sacred Text or a psalm to rouse the spirit: Come, let us adore.

Some may find it of value and profit to have a more significant vigil once or twice a week, perhaps on Thursday night with Jesus in Gethsemane. This could take the form of rising a good bit earlier, sacrificing some sleep this one night; or breaking sleep at the seventh hour to join in spirit with the monks and nuns in their monasteries. This might be easier on a Friday night or early Saturday morning, when it would be possible to return to bed for a longer sleep. Missing sleep is not the important thing, though for some this can be a significant ascetical dimension of the practice. More important is the experience of being vigilant in the dark silence when others are not commonly abroad and even the creation has a certain dormancy. There is something about the deepness of that bottoming of nature's daily cycle (even in the city where it might still be punctuated by police sirens, the clatter of garbage collectors, and the fights of alley cats) that opens out the deeper recesses of the spirit and lets its truer language surface. At such an hour what does creation do but await the sun? What can we do but await the Son?

> I wait for Yahweh, my soul waits for him,—more than a watchman waits for the dawn. (Ps. 130:5–6)

The spirit of watching can be carried on beyond the actual time of prayer. As we shower, shave, and dress we can continue to meditate on some Scripture text, repeat some simple prayer, or simply abide in the Presence, longing for an ever greater presence. A household agreement that allows this to be a time of quiet without chatter, or the blare of radio, stereo, or television would greatly facilitate this. The watch could formally be concluded with a bit of family prayer at the breakfast table. In my Uncle Clark's home we had a psalm with a moment's reflection and a spontaneous prayer before we dived into our breakfast.

In reading the Fathers of the Church and our twelfth-century Cistercian Fathers, we repeatedly come upon the statement: "One who has experienced this understands what I am talking about; one who has not, let him seek the experience and then he will understand." When I was a young monk I used to be quite annoyed when I came upon such "snobbish" statements. Now I begin to understand. Anyone who has loved will. Just try to get another to understand what you experience in being with your loved one! The same is true here.

The value and effect of watching can only be known by experience. Even a little watching done *regularly* not only reveals its own significance, but has an effect on one's whole life. In the watching, new dimensions of the soul's natural magnetism toward the Lord begin to reveal themselves, and the soul begins to have the joy of drawing the Lord into its cool darkness, radiating the warmth of unseen light. At the same time a certain integrity and unity seems gradually to take more and more hold of the multitudinous strands of life, creating a satisfying and empowering harmony. The whole comes more and more into harmony. The reasons for this could be explored at length: a purification process is being facilitated. As the solitary watching opens deeper places to healing love, a sensitive perception is becoming more penetrating as these deeper openings are illuminated by the dark light; a freer, more vigorous spirit that has been strengthened to stand its ground in the struggle with darkness takes a firmer hold on the direction of one's life. The extensive effect of a relatively little investment of yourself and your time in watching will in many ways be surprising. The experience of it is in itself very rewarding, and it is a constantly growing experience for those who are faithful to the practice.

Watch—and you will see!

Be Still ...

The sun would soon rest on the horizon. The flood tide of a day's activities is ebbing. A calm enfolds the abbey as a great cowl. The monks silently gather in the reading cloister along the south wall of the church. A junior reads a few pages from the sayings of the desert fathers:

> Theophilus of holy memory, Bishop of Alexandria journeyed to Scete, and the brethren coming together said to Abbot Pambo: Say a word or two to the Bishop, that his soul may be edified in this place. The elder replied: If he is not edified by my silence, there is no hope he will be edified by my words.

Tu autem. The abbot gives the signal to conclude the reading: "And you . . . Lord, have mercy on us." The "Thanks be to God," comes from deep within the monks. Another day is drawing to a close—a blessed day for his mercy has been with them. They silently file into the church and into their stalls. The bell rings and the ancient service of Compline proceeds. Finally, the lights fade. Two solitary candles shadow the folds of her mantle and caress the smooth cheeks of the medieval Madonna, the Queen of Citeaux. And the monks' voices rise in the plaintiff chant:

> Hail, Holy Queen, Mother of Mercy, our life, our sweetness, and our hope . . . O clement, O loving, O sweet Virgin, Mary.

The final strokes of the angelus bell lose themselves in the surrounding hills. The monks bow, one by one, to be washed again with the baptismal waters and sent into the night with their abbot's blessing. Night has come. The "great silence" has taken hold of the abbey:

> At all times monks ought to strive to keep silence but particularly so during the hours of the night, and this means in all seasons, whether on days of fasting or on days of having a midday meal. If it is the latter season, then after rising from supper, they should at once sit together and one of them should read the *Conferences* or the *Lives of the Fathers* . . . So when all are assembled, they should say Compline, and when they come out of Compline there should be no further permission for anyone to talk about anything.

Creation has given up its activities and is hushed. It is time for the monk who has entered into God's established rhythm to be quiet and rest.

When we think of monks, we think of silence. I cannot say how many times I have been asked: Do you still have a vow of silence? Actually Trappists have never taken a vow of silence. Few monks have. Perhaps the most famous is the great icon painter Roublev. It was during fourteen years of vowed silence that he produced some of his greatest works. Silence had released his creative genius.

We do not have a vow of silence but we do have important rules of silence in the monastery. They are essential if a group of persons is going to live together and still have the context in which to seek truly.

One of my favorite biblical scenarios (I have many) concerns the holy prophet Elijah, the patron of our Byzantine chapel. He was a sporting man and challenged the false prophets of Baal to a contest. They gathered on Mount Carmel, each with his altar and holocaust. The Baalites cried all day for fire from heaven and Elijah goaded them on with his stinging jibes. Needless to say, no fire came. Then Elijah soaked his offering and altar with water and filled the trench around it with more of the same. Then he raised a single cry to heaven. Fire not only consumed the holocaust, it took the altar, too, and lapped up all the water in the trench. The crowd was ecstatic, and encouraged by the holy prophet, proceeded to slit the throats of the false prophets. A bit of excess, we might say. The queen felt that way, and promised Elijah the same. He made for the desert. A discouraged man—his great triumph had landed him in exile—he lay beneath a scrubby tree and complained to God as he fell into sleep. The Lord had something to teach his sporting prophet. An angel poked him, fueled him up, and sent him on a forty-day trek to the holy mountain of Horeb. The prophet found himself a cave and waited upon the Lord. A mighty wind tore the mountain and shattered the rocks. But the Lord God was not in the wind. There was a violent earthquake and Elijah shook. But the Lord God was not in the

earthquake. Fire blazed up, and around, and came down.
But the Lord God was not in the fire. Then came a sound
as if a gentle breeze.

> When Elijah heard this, he covered his face with his
> cloak and went out and stood at the entrance of the
> cave.

The Lord God was in the gentle breeze, in the sounds of
silence. Elijah learned to cloak himself in silence to hear
the Lord. This is the deepest reason for the monk's silence,
whether it be the "great silence" of the night which enfolds his sleep and his watching or the spaces and places of
silence he guards in the day. It is to hear God. It is to tune
out others for the moment so he can tune in God. "Be
still, and know that I am God."

God does indeed speak to us through all the events of
life, through all the persons we encounter. He is actually in
the mighty wind, the earthquake, the fire, in all. But we
will not hear him in any of these—not even in the voice
and embrace of a lover, if in the silence we have not
learned the sound of his voice. It is very subtle, even
though it thunders louder than all the voices of his creation. Two could be sitting in the warm sun, as I am now,
listening to the bright morning calls of chickadees, robins,
finches, and sparrows. One might only hear the rich melo-
dies, while the other, who perhaps had sat that morning in
the silence and had attuned his inner ear to the divine
voice, hears a message of ineffable love: Listen to the birds
of the air. They do not sow or reap or gather into barns;
yet your heavenly Father feeds them. You are worth much
more than they. You are held in an infinite caring love.

In the silence, whether we listen to the creation around us, the words of revelation, or the deepest stirrings of our own hearts, we begin to perceive another voice, one that is too often lost in the static of life. It is no use saying: "Speak, Lord, your servant wants to hear," if we never risk the silence to listen. If we never sit still we will never perceive the gentle breezes that caress our necks and kiss our cheeks with love—a divine love.

In the spaces of silence the monk hears God, is embraced by God, delights in God. No wonder he is a lover of silence. He also hears someone else. He hears himself—his true self.

I have repeatedly said that happiness consists in knowing what you want and then knowing you have it or are on the way to getting it. Most people are unhappy because they do not know what they want. This not knowing is partially a failure to choose. God does give us an immense amount of options from which we can choose. Some refuse to choose or find themselves paralyzed in the face of choice, because to choose one means to give up in some way all the others. But even those who do choose are often unhappy because the choice is not responsive to their own deepest needs and desires. We have to know ourselves in order to know what we want. Ultimately, it is only when we see ourselves reflected back in the all-loving eyes of God, when we hear him speak our name, do we truly know ourselves with our infinite potential for beauty, for life, for truth, for love. It is only then that we know our own awesome beauty, that we are worthy of the divine love because he has made us worthy. Only then do we know that "our hearts are made for you, O Lord, and they will not rest until they rest in you." In silence we come to know ourselves and know what we truly want. And the doorway to happiness opens.

Unfortunately, in seeing ourselves as we truly are, not all that we see is beautiful and attractive. This is undoubtedly part of the reason we flee silence. We do not want to be confronted with our hypocrisy, our phoniness. We see how false and fragile is the false self we project. We have to go through this painful experience to come to our true self. It is a harrowing journey, a death to self—the false self—and no one wants to die. But it is the only path to life, to freedom, to peace, to true love. And it begins with silence. We cannot give ourselves in love if we do not know and possess ourselves. This is the great value of silence. It is the pathway to all we truly want. This is why Saint Benedict speaks of silence as if it were a value in itself: for the sake of silence.

He notes, too, another aspect, quoting Sacred Scripture: "In a flood of word you will not avoid sin." Good communication is beautiful; it is precious. It is also relatively rare. If we feel we must fill all the time we have with others with chatter and even all the time alone with the sounds of radio or television or our own productions, we will be filled with lots of useless and even harmful words, thoughts, sounds, and ideas. And our own contribution will be lacking in quality to say the least. How quickly we descend to gossip, to detraction, to calumny. To be together in the silence listening to the many messages of divine love, to the message of divine love that we are to each other, can bond a relationship and be a far more meaningful and fruitful communication than most of our speech.

Some years ago we received into our community for a week eleven Methodist ministers. As they were giving us feedback at the end of the experience the input of one of them touched me deeply. He said he was awed by the respect and trust we showed each other in the way we were together in the silence. The others agreed.

We do have rules of silence in the monastery. There are times of silence: the "great silence" of the night, the times of prayer, study, reading, and rest. And there are places of silence: the cloisters, the reading rooms, the cell, and . . . These are essential if we are to live together in freedom. We have to have our mutual understandings and our commitment to them. If you want the value of silence in your life you will have to find or create places of silence, you will have to agree on times of silence. It might be an hour or two in the evening or a few hours on Sunday afternoon when each is left free to read and pray, reflect and write. This is not impossible with children. They can be put to quiet games with themselves with their coloring books or blocks. For teenagers whose lives are encased in the ceaseless blare of a sound called music, to be given a structure to discover silence, to discover their true selves in a daily dose of silence, can be a gift that is perhaps at first not welcomed, but for which, as for dry wine, a taste develops that will last for a lifetime. The individuality of all children should, of course be respected. If they cannot enter into the silence, they should be asked at least to respect the needs of others. Modeling by parents in this regard as so many others is very important. The basic human need for balance between auditory stimulation and silence can be missed, becoming an unknown cause of much stress and strain.

As I have said, a sort of great silence in the home till the family gathers at the breakfast table can allow the daily routine of morning exercises, showering, shaving, and dressing to become part of the watch in the night, a time for *lectio* and prayer. If we take a word from Scripture upon arising, it can be an accompaniment through the morning rituals and a touch-point for the whole day. To take a couple of minutes when we first get out of bed to receive the rising sun or the setting stars can bring peace to the whole day. To take time to center for fifteen or twenty minutes after our exercises and shower can put us deeply in touch with God and self and solidly ground all the activities of our day, till we collect them all into the center at evening meditation.

The other side of silence is communication. These two are not wholly distinct. We can communicate by silence. Some of our best communication is in silence. Indeed as we have said, the primary purpose of silence is communication, to truly hear God, to hear ourselves and others, and the whole creation more deeply. But there is a time to communicate in words, one of our precious prerogatives. True communication is perhaps as rare or rarer than true silence. It, too, can and often times should be fostered by some structures. Monasticism has its chapter meetings, its spiritual fathers and mothers, its traditional teaching on spiritual friendship. Marriage Encounter has offered the practical tool of ten and ten. The spouses are asked each day to spend ten minutes writing to each other and ten minutes talking to each other of their relationship. Families need to schedule family meetings and decide really to talk to each other about the things that flow out of their being family. Busy friends have to make time to be together in silence and in honest communication. There is a time for us to sit mentally with each friend, each member of our family, each member of our community, so that all can speak their being to us and we can check our response of love and care. I do this on my monthly retreat day.

Actually, true communication does not interrupt silence. As Thomas Kelly, speaking from Quaker silence, has so beautifully put it: "Words should not break silence, but continue it. For the Divine Life who was ministering through the medium of silence is the same Life as is now ministering through words." To put it another way, whether we be silent or whether we speak, it is the Divine Word we want to hear and to express. This is the silence of the cloister that is so full of love, joy, and peace, of the presence of the Holy Spirit. "In silence, you shall gain your soul" and all else besides.

A Complete "Yes"

It has been customary for Catholic writers to add a chapter on Mary at the end of their books on Christian life, as has, for example, the popular liberation theologian, Segundo Galileo, in his beautiful study, *Following Jesus*. (Mary is the greatest follower of Jesus and hence a model for us in this.) I have done this regularly myself. But here I place it to the fore. I hope this is not ecumenically offensive. I am certainly not saying Mary is first. Jesus is first, Jesus our God. But God—the Christian God (if we may use such an expression), the Father, revealed through Jesus Christ—first came to us in Mary and through Mary. The Good News was first announced explicitly to her. In its earliest prophetic announcement it was associated with her:

> Then Yahweh God said to the serpent . . . "I will make you enemies of each other: you and the woman, your offspring and her offspring."
>
> Genesis 3:14–15

The Lord himself, therefore, will give you a sign. It is
this: the maiden is with child and will soon give
birth to a son whom she will call Immanuel.

Isaiah 7:14

For Yahweh is creating something new on earth: the
Woman sets out to find her Husband again.

Jeremiah 31:22

In Byzantine architecture the royal doors separate the
holy place from the nave of the church, reminiscent of the
veil of the temple in Jerusalem. But unlike the veil, which
hid a place of fullest but unrevealed mystery and therefore
hung in transcendent silence, the royal doors which open
to bring forth the Incarnate God in sacred Communion
set forth the images of the bearers of the Good News. The
four Evangelists are depicted on their respective panels.
Over and above them is Gabriel bearing the glad tidings to
Mary, the Maiden. Mary was the first to receive the Good
News of the incarnation, and in receiving it and accepting
it, in God's design she helped to bring it about. Christ-
God received his incarnation, his humanity, his blood relationship with us in and through her.

Saint Leo the Great (+461), sharing the voice of the
Fathers of the Church, tells us that Mary in becoming the
mother of the Head (taking up the Pauline theology of
the Mystical Body of Christ) mothered also all his
members. Some of the Fathers have used the less gracious
image of the neck—Mary is the "neck" of the Mystical
Body. What they are saying is that all that comes to us
from Christ, the Head of the Body, comes to us through

Mary, the neck of the Body. Mary is the mediatrix of all graces. She was the way by which our Mediator descended from heaven to us. She collaborated with him in the first hours of his salvific mission and has never left off that collaboration. All from Jesus through Mary.

Monks have always been men of their times, even while they stepped outside of their times in quest of the transcendent and eternal. The medieval Cistercians were no exception. And their Marian piety is marked by the social structures and outlook of that period. Knowing that all comes through Mary, they saw their monasteries as belonging to her as their Lady, the Mother and Consort of their Lord. All their monasteries bore her name, along with that of the locale: the Monastery of Blessed Mary of the Valley of Light (Clairvaux); the Monastery of Blessed Mary of the Beautiful Fountain (Bellefontaine); the Monastery of Blessed Mary of the Seven Fountains (Sept Fons). The monks—when they entered the monastic community and took up residence in her house—became her vassals and took her name, usually along with that of one of her great servants. In acknowledgment of their filial fiefdom, each evening they ended their day's service with the solemn chant, "Hail, Holy Queen." These practices continue to be a part of the living heritage of the Cistercian monks of today in all parts of the world.

I have known Mary as my Mother since I first came to know her at my mother's knee. My earthly mother, now in heaven, told me of my heavenly Mother and was a sacrament of her love and care. Grandma taught me the rosary at an early age. The beads I had seen so often in her fingers had fascinated me. In the school of the rosary I came to know my Mother, and in the May and October devotions, and in the living of the liturgical year from the feast of the Immaculate Conception and the birth of the Virgin, to the Annunciation, Visitation, and Nativity, and on through the Passion to the glories of the Assumption. In the monastery liturgical readings and personal *lectio* brought me the reflective faith and rich theology of the Fathers and the monastic tradition. I came to know more (and it is still growing) the sublimity of "our tainted nature's solitary boast." I experienced more her mediation and in this her intimate closeness. Her virginal freedom and complete dispossessiveness that enabled her to be pure gift have called me. Her brave exile has encouraged me in my going apart from others. Her unjust persecution with her hunted Son and her identification with the condemned crucified One, have enabled me to accept the daily contradictions and to identify more fully with my persecuted and suffering brothers and sisters. This complete "yes" constantly challenges me. I want—by her example and mediation—to be like her Son, a "yes" to the Father.

I put these pages on Mary first in this book to acknowledge that all that I have, all that I am, all that I can share in this volume, comes from God, from the God-Man, our Lord Jesus, through Mary. In a most special way I belong to her.

I come from a largely Protestant background. Members of my family belong to many different Christian churches. Some of them do not understand or see Mary's role as I do. But I think, and hope I am right in saying, that we all can respect each other's understanding and perceive the beauty and integrity that calls each one of us to believe and live faithfully as we do.

The fact that our monasteries actually belong to Mary is concretely acknowledged by the presence of her image—a window, statue, or painting—in a most prominent place in the church, usually above the principal altar. As the day's services conclude, candles are lit before the image and all other lights fade out. For a few moments all attention is focused on Mary, and one of the most solemn, beautiful, and beloved chants, the "Salve Regina" (Hail, Queen Mother) is sung to her. Then, for the third time in the course of the day, a special bell calls us to a special prayer.

There are in our belfry three bells. They are the gift of a Congregational minister, a memorial to his son, a victim of the hatred that is war. These bells now call us to the peace of prayer. The great one, well over a ton, is Joseph's, the man who cared for Mary as a husband. The second is Bernard's, the mystic of the Valley of Light, who wrote—no, sang, of Mary in prose as no other ever has. And the third, the highest and the sweetest, is Mary's. It now rings out in three strokes of three. Each time this happens in the monastic day, all comes to a standstill in the abbey. All face the church; some stand, some kneel, some prostrate. And we live again in sacramental mystery that most awesome moment in salvation history, when

> The angel of the Lord declared unto Mary,
> And she conceived of the Holy Spirit.
>> (Reflect for the space of an *Ave*—Hail Mary.)
> Behold the Handmaid of the Lord,

Be it done unto me according to your word.
     (Reflection)
The Word was made flesh
And dwelt among us.
     (Reflection)

And then as the bell rings out, we pray:

Pray for us, O holy Mother of God,
That we may be made worthy of the promises of
Christ.

Pour forth, we beseech you, O Lord, your grace into
our hearts, that we to whom the Incarnation of Christ
your Son was made known by the message of an
angel, may by his passion and death be brought to the
glory of his resurrection. Through the same Christ,
our Lord. Amen.

The bell falls silent, the prayer is completed. The monks
file silently toward the dormitory stairs. A very perceptive
observer can notice a certain stirring within the monks'
long sleeves and perhaps hear a gentle rattle of beads. As
they go about the monastery, most often monks finger the
beads—Mary's rosary.

Some of the most beautiful images I have of my
brothers arise now. I think of old Brother Alfred, ninety
years young, shuffling down the road all but hidden under
his broad-brimmed straw hat, a sturdy cane in one hand
and the rosary prominently in the other. Indeed, I can
hardly remember a time when I have met Brother and he
did not have the rosary in hand. Brother Stan, our Polish

wrestler, was the same, his rosary so full of medals, we could always hear him coming.

The rosary stays in the monk's hand as he falls off to sleep. It is often in his hand during the day as he prays and meditates. He trusts it will be in his hand when Mary prays for him "at the hour of our death," and his brothers lay him gently on the boughs of spruce at the bottom of his grave.

Each home can certainly profit not only by a dedication that will place it securely under the special care of the Mother of all, but by her presence therein, symbolized by a worthy shrine. Those who enter the home of a devout Orthodox Christian are immediately greeted by the holy icons enshrined in the corner facing the entry. They bring a real Presence to the home and family and all visitors. Mary's image can do the same for us. Such a presence will invite the family at significant moments—how good it would be if it were each evening—to gather around. The house and all its blessings come from God through her. From her comes the strength to bear the burdens and trials. She, the Mother, can gather the children together when humanness drives them apart. She can watch over those absent, far or near.

There can, of course, be other times and places of prayer and gratitude. In the home of one of my brothers, grace at table always ends ". . . through Christ, our Lord, and his Immaculate Mother." The Angelus, that thrice daily commemoration of the Incarnation, is an especially beautiful practice. While thanking God for this most precious of all his gifts, I find my own hope, confidence, and joy, constantly renewed by this prayer. It is something different each time. It is a touching of the substance of what is. Not to allow ourselves these moments open to the fulfillment of all we long for and desire, not to structure such moments into our daily lives, is to cheat ourselves of so much that is rightfully ours.

And then there are the "beads," the rosary. It doesn't take long to pray the rosary—ten or fifteen minutes is ample. But we don't have to wait till we have even that bit of time. If we carry the beads in a pocket or keep them nearby, we can finger them any free moment. As the monk prays his beads while walking down the cloister or the path to work or upstairs, so the beads can be the prayer of passing moments. In fact, no word need be said, nor specific thought—the touch of the fingers can be the silent heart-felt outreach to God through and with Mary.

As we pray the rosary more formally, we ponder the most intimate mysteries of our faith-life, with the Hail Mary as the quiet background. We ask Mary to lead us into that fullness of understanding that she ultimately found, through a lived participation, and into that full sharing of the fruit of these saving mysteries that is preeminently hers in her complete freedom from sin and her corporeal glorification in the palace of her Son.

Mary is first because she sought to be last. Behold the handmaid, the servant, the slave girl, the one unworthy of motherhood. The monk seeks a way of life that is to be characterized, as Saint Benedict, the holy father of the monastic way, puts it, by zeal for *opprobria*—a desire for the humble and humbling way, so that he might mother Christ the better in himself and others. If we would be close to Mary in her greatest and her greatness, we must be close to her in her lowliness. The life of each one of us is marked with the daily cross: pains, aches, humiliations . . . Mary points the hopeful way to rise from these with her Risen Son so that we might, with her, ascend to him in glory.

Fasting
A Hunger for Freedom

From the fourteenth of September until the beginning of Lent let the monks take their meal in the middle of the afternoon. In Lent, however, they will dine after Vespers.

—Saint Benedict's *Rule for Monasteries*

The great monastic legislator of the West has been reputed for his moderation, but the regime he spells out for his monks with regard to fasting sounds anything but moderate to many of us moderns: one meal a day most of the year, and that in late afternoon or evening. For the time and the place, though, and in comparison with the feats of his monastic forebears, this is moderate indeed.

At one time Abba Agathon had two disciples, each leading the anchoritic life according to his own measure. One day he asked the first: "How do you live in the cell?" He replied: "I fast until evening, then I eat two hard biscuits." He said to him, "Your way of life is good, not overburdened with too much asceticism."

Then he asked the other one: "And you, how do you live?" He replied: "I fast for two days, then I eat two hard biscuits."

* * *

Abba Abraham went to see Abba Ares. They were sitting together when a brother came to the old man and said to him, "Tell me what I must do to be saved." He replied, "Go, and for the whole of this year eat only bread and salt in the evening. Then come back here and I will talk to you again." The monk went away and did this. When the year was over he came back to Abba Ares. Now by chance it happened that Abba Abraham was there again. Once more the old man said to the brother, "Go, and for the whole of this year fast for two days at a time."

But the Fathers moved toward moderation:

Abba Joseph said to Abba Poemen, "When you were younger, did you not fast two days at a time, Abba?" The old man said, "Yes, even for three days and four and the whole week. The Fathers tried all this out as they were able and they found it preferable to eat every day, but just a small amount. They left us this royal way, which is light."

Benedict's rule, then, of one meal a day was no departure from the tradition. But the temperate legislator did temper its rigor. There was, of course, no fast during the holy Paschal season nor on the day of Resurrection, Sunday. Such a fast would be heretical. The Bridegroom is with his Church. It is no time for fasting but only for a wedding feast. With Pentecost the fast can return, but Benedict would limit it to two days a week, and even these would be dispensed with if the heat or the summer labors would make a fast too burdensome.

When the monastic fast was resumed in the fall, Abba Benedict was loath to prescribe a precise regime: "Each has his own proper gift from God: one this, one that. And therefore it is with some diffidence that a measure of food is established by us." At all meals there are to be two cooked portions, so that if a monk cannot eat of the one he at least has the other. If the work is heavy, more is to be given. If the garden offers it, salad and fruit are added. Even though tradition proscribed wine for monks, Benedict bends to the custom of his time and country and allows a healthy portion. He warns only against overdoing things and invites the monks to do more on their own, especially during Lent.

Benedict's true disciples have always held fasting in high regard. Mitigations have come in through the centuries. When they are in response to real need they are fully legitimate, for the wise legislator always left it to the discretion of the local abbot to adapt his Rule to the circumstances. But "frugality should be the rule on all occasions"—a frugality that left the tummy grumbling at times. As one of Benedict's later disciples, the twelfth-century Cistercian Isaac of Stella, put it: "The man who eats whenever he is hungry doesn't have any idea what a fast is. The virtue and merit of fasting begin only when one is hungry." Fasting really counts only when one hungers, and the longer this endures, the more the fast counts.

That is Isaac's brief word on fasting, at least on physical

fasting. But he immediately goes on to say: "There is another more sacred and higher type of fasting." Those who have entered into the solitude of the spirit are to observe it carefully and diligently, and constantly, too, all the days of their lives, in times of prosperity and in times of adversity, whether one be a superior or a subject, whether engaged in contemplation or activity. And this fast is the fast from the delights and consolations of this world.

In a previous sermon Isaac spoke of another kind of spiritual fast: "This is the fast which the Lord chooses: to abstain from all evil, not only in external works, but also interiorly from evil desires." However, even as he sets before us this ideal of the monastic life, Isaac is not lacking in that full Christian humanism, the true incarnationalism that marks the whole Cistercian school. He readily sees and openly declares: Man cannot live without pleasure. But the spiritual man is to find his delight and consolation in the Lord: *Memor fui Dei et delectatus sum.* His delightful nourishment is found in meditations, prayer, communion with the Lord.

Fasting is a life attitude and its significance lies in establishing that kind of relationship with the Creator that it serves the main thrust of Christian life—the desire for union and fullness of life in Christ. In his chapter on Lent, Saint Benedict writes:

> . . . each one may offer up to God in the joy of the Holy Spirit something over and above the measure appointed him: that is, let him deny his body in food, in drink, in sleep, in superfluous talking and mirth, and withal long for the holy feast of Easter with the joy of holy desire.

A physical emptiness and hunger supports a spirtual hunger, a hunger for God.

Fasting is an attitude of life marked by joy because it is a stance toward Creator and creation that is dictated by the desires of love. Such an attitude is wholly foreign to anything picayune, though nothing is so small as not to merit its due appreciation and place. It is not at all tied up with little rules and regulations, yet it does not fail to appreciate the human imperative of incarnation and communal order and expression. There is a time, and there needs to be a time, when the Christian community, whether it be the cellular local community or one of the larger components of the whole worldwide Christian body, together affirms in a coordinated and significant way (by a sign that speaks) its adhesion to the rules inherent in fasting. Every community and every household should be aware of this. One of the things sapping Christian life today is the failure to incarnate our values in ways that witness to our membership and allow for a healthy experience of our basic unities.

As Christians, one of the basic reasons for adopting this attitude toward life, and the source of our perceiving its values, is our devotion to Christ and our adherence to him as Master. We want to be Christ's disciples and follow in his way, the way to fuller, risen life.

Christ's forty days in the desert, with its almost total fast from the presence and use of the things of creation, is very striking. It underlies the value of an occasional radical withdrawal from the use and enjoyment of things and even from the society of friends, especially as a preparation for a significant undertaking.

But Christ's whole life was marked with a certain sobriety in his use of things. As he tramped the roads on his life's mission he did not keep any comfortable nest to return to. "The Son of Man has not whereon to lay his head." He took things as he found them, made do (sleeping in the boat, for example, or at Peter's house), depended on his Father, shared with his friends, receiving their everyday care and benefactions and coming up with his own miraculous spread on occasion. He got along frugally, but there was time for the splurge of the Passover feast. And a party at Levi's or Simon's was not turned down.

Most basic was his attitude to his Father in all. How many times did he say, "I thank you, Father"; how many times did he raise his eyes to heaven to bless God!

Not only as loving disciples of Christ, desirous of having his mind and heart, but as beloved children of the Father, gratitude shown by appreciation must mark our response to creation. Has not each one of us, at one time or another, known the pain of ingratitude when we have seen our gift lying broken and dusty in the corner, or in the trash can seen something that we esteemed at a price, wantonly wasted by a thoughtless recipient? All that we have, all that we are, is the gracious gift of our Father. The realization of this is the basis for a true ecology. The gift in itself is precious. But how much more value is added to it by our love for the Giver! How offensive to him is a wanton, wasteful or useless consumption or destruction of his precious gifts! Love for the Father inspires us to hold each bit of creation as precious and to use it with due care.

None of us is an "only child." Christ is the firstborn of

many brethren. We have a whole world of brothers and sisters, and many more to come. The Father's gifts are meant for all of us, to provide for the needs of all, and for the good pleasure and life-enrichment of us all. We are bound to one another by our common needs. We all need to eat. We all need to drink. We all need to be clothed. All of us—not just a few! The ages yet to come—not just this generation. And so, with love, we take care. We gratefully use what we need. We enjoy what is present to us. We try to see that all have the joy of sharing with us in this banquet of creation. And in this sharing our joy is multiplied. Only the glutton can enjoy gorging himself alone. Even the hermit finds joy in knowing that the bit he is using is a sharing from the common table of man. When we fast and know the pangs of hunger we are in compassionate communion with our desperately hungry brothers and sisters in the ghettos and Appalachias of our own country as well as in the blighted corners and expanses of our globe. Out of the emptiness of each of us as individuals comes a fullness of all of us together.

Such privation does not really impoverish us. It is not necessary for us to consume created goods or to grasp them in material possession in order to be aggrandized by them. No. In fact, a greedy consumption or a grasping subjection only impoverishes creation and reduces its potential to enrich us. It is only when we truly reverence the created and allow its goodness to speak to us in its own right that it can most fully bestow on us its richness—its share of the divine goodness and beauty.

As the glutton gulps down his carrots, he gets his proteins, carbohydrates, and calories and a passing feeling of being full, but it is all so passing—except the unwanted calories! But one who has a reverent attitude of grateful appreciation can well be filled with the wonder of the carrot, and savor its unique flavor, texture, color, and odor—truly enjoy it and be nourished by it in spirit as well as body. The grasping possessor reduces all he grasps to the sole value that inspires his grasping—dollars and cents, power, prestige, sensual satisfaction. The reverent and grateful recipient lets each thing express to him all its own unique values of goodness and beauty as well as the overwhelming love of the Giver.

A fasting attitude multiplies the enrichment while it minimizes the consumption. And it gives birth to freedom.

We are poor, needy creatures, ever hanging on the mercy of God and of our fellow-travelers on this planet Earth. Yet how many of our experienced needs are truly needs? How much is our bondage multiplied by pseudo-needs—those "needs" that come from Madison Avenue brainwashing or our own enslavement to habitude? How freeing can be an experience of radical fasting from food when it teaches us in our guts that we can indeed survive and survive quite well without three squares a day and so many calories, proteins, and carbohydrates. And this is without yet considering the expansion of spiritual horizons that arises in us when we enjoy a period of significant abstinence from food and drink.

So it is, too, with watching in the night, after the initial struggle, when an experience of the restorative power of deep prayer frees us from the psychological dependency on so many hours of sleep. I could go on and on. We can learn the freedom of getting along with less clothing, less heat, less sound to fill our silences, less objects to fill our spaces, less diversions to fill our time. The little, when given a chance to blossom and express all its own proper reality, can with its beauty fill to overflowing all our capacities. For each speck of creation is not only the gift of the Father, but a participation in his very being with all its beauty. This is the joy about which Saint Benedict is speaking.

As we grow in gratitude and appreciation we need less and less of creation; we are freer and freer to find in ourselves and in the expansive little we already have, all that we want and need. This is why the poor can be the happiest. They have the freedom to enjoy fully all they have. Those who possess more must expend time and energy taking care of their many things, to the extent that they have not the time to enjoy any of them freely and fully. Somoza possessed a large portion of the land in Nicaragua, yet he was said to be terribly jealous of the poor and persecuted them because they seemed to enjoy his land more than he did. Such men lose their freedom and become the servants or even the slaves of what they are said to possess. They do not possess—they are possessed.

Indeed we can all ask ourselves as we look around at the clutter of our own lives, great or little as it might be, and look at our habitudes: Do I possess or am I possessed? Do I use or am I used? Is this what Paul was talking about when he said we should use this creation as if we used it not? To be able to use the good things of our Father's beneficence and enjoy them in such a way that we retain our ability to use them not, to get along without them— this is true freedom.

Fasting in our time has taken on some new social dimensions, most significantly through Mahatma Gandhi. It always had social dimensions for monks. The Fathers of the Egyptian desert deprived themselves of food and sent boatloads of grain down the river to feed the poor of Alexandria. Through the ages, whatever remained over at the table of the monks was taken to the gate to be shared with the poor. Just last year I saw this being done in an Indian monastery. Where this is not feasible, monks have held their special days of fast, feasting on bread and water or a bowl of rice in solidarity with the world's hungry, and sending a check for what the regular meals would have cost to someone who could immediately care for the needy. But with Gandhi, fasting became a means to underline a cause, to proclaim that the attainment of certain values has more meaning than life itself, that for such values it is worth laying down one's life. Such a fast can unfortunately be easily and subtlely diverted from proclamation to weapon, from non-violence to violence.

One of Gandhi's rules for public fasting was that it "cannot be resorted to against those who regard us as their enemy, or on whose love we have not established a claim by dint of selfless service." But as proclamation it is in accord with the monastic tradition. For surely the monks' fast did proclaim an allegiance to values higher than sustaining physical life at its maximum. The tradition never espoused a fast unto death, and indeed, fasting seems to have fostered longevity in monasteries, but it did affirm that, for a follower of Christ, there are values greater than physical well-being.

Perhaps not much needs to be said by way of practical

suggestion for integrating fasting into one's life in the everyday world. The moderation of Saint Benedict is generally to be espoused. Times and seasons of more fasting are good when done with counsel. The saintly legislator would have his monks get the abbot's approval for all their Lenten extras. Each, according to health and labors, will have to find his or her own measure. Christ's disciples do fast in the absence of the Bridegroom. A weekly fast day, whatever the measure may be—a complete fast, a water fast, or simply depriving oneself of dessert, would seem to be a good general rule. Except, of course, during the holy Easter season.

Where a question does frequently arise today is in regard to the relation or possible relation between fasting and dieting. Some look askance at the person who proclaims as the goal of his Lenten fast to lose twenty-three pounds. I would not. In fact, I would see a certain lack of integration in the outlook that would necessarily dichotomize fasting and dieting. Saint Paul tells us: "Whether you eat or drink or whatever else you do, do all for the glory of God." Dieting is one of those "whatever elses" we do. We can not-eat and not-drink for the glory of God. Certainly, taking good care of our bodies, of our health, is something God wants us to do. And this can demand dieting. The immediate effect of fasting and dieting can be the same; the immediate purpose is not; but the further purpose can be, and the ultimate purpose, the glory of God, should be.

A fast is called a diet when its immediate purpose is perfecting the body. A diet is a fast when its immediate purpose is a spiritual good: to mitigate the hold of the body, to attain freedom for the spirit and clarity for the mind, to proclaim higher values. There is nothing contradictory here; both purposes can be simultaneously sought. If people are going to diet, they would be wise to seek the spiritual benefits along with the physical, and certainly the diet should be integrated into one's overall life of love of God and neighbor.

Saint Bernard, in a beautiful treatise, *On the Love of God*, tells us there are four degrees of love. The first is self-love, actually the love of a false or superficial self. The second is a love of God which is motivated by the benefits we receive from him. We love God because he is good to us, or we perceive that this is the only way to find happiness. In this we are servants acting for gain; it is a mercenary love. The third degree of love is to love God because he is lovable, truly worthy of all love. It is the love of a lover. We love him and in that love forget ourselves. This is true love. Finally, Bernard postulates a fourth degree of love: we love ourselves because of the love of God. We so love God that we identify wholly with him and love all he loves. Among the things he loves, of course, is ourselves. We are good and lovable because he has made us so; we are his image and likeness, we are his creation. This is indeed true love of self, love of our true self. Out of such a love we can be called to diet and to fast. Indeed, when motivated by such a love, every diet would seem to have to be a fast, but we might be called to a fast that goes beyond dieting, to deprive ourselves to a point where the body does suffer some diminution of its well-being.

I am afraid this has gotten rather complex in the state-ment. In practice, simplicity can cut right through it. No matter what dietary regimen we follow or how we use the rest of God's gifts, we can seek to do it for love of him and for love of our true selves, seeking to be free from the bur-den of overweight, sluggishness, addictive appetites or any greedy possessiveness—and letting this be the norm for the way we practically act. Freedom to be fully who we want to be, to be who God wants us to be, should be the motive and norm of our dieting and fasting—freedom to be pure love. Monastic tradition would speak of this as achieving purity of heart.

A life marked by an attitude of fasting, a life that retains the freedom to use only what it really needs, and use that little with reverence and gratitude toward the Father, in imitation of Christ, is not then an impoverished life, but one open to the fullest enrichment. An attitude of Christ-like fasting certainly does not mean less esteem for the good of created things; no, it means a greater esteem for them as gifts of the Father. It does not mean distancing ourselves from created things but actually getting closer to them. For we perceive more their true goodness and in our appreciation take them into ourselves more fully and at a level more consonant with their true nature as partici-pations of the Divine All-good and with our true nature as persons of spirit as well as body.

Fasting is a true human good. Many today are more aware of this and are trying to experience it more in all sorts of experiments at communal or eremitical living. Many are being drawn to its strongly evocative presence among the devotees of Eastern religions. Yet for us, the disciples of Christ, the attitude of fasting and the living out of it has been elevated, divinized, made fraternal and filial in the example of our Divine Master. Should not our lives be joyfully illumined and shine forth with this, the good of Christian fasting?

Hearing the Word of God
and Keeping It:
The Benedictine Method

Father Anthony de Mello, one of India's leading spiritual teachers today, in his work *Sadhana: A Way to God*, offers many simple methods spiritual teachers can use to help their disciples learn to pray. The thirty-second method he offers is called "The Benedictine Method." His presentation is well done, concise, clear, and quite complete. The fact that it is thirty-second helps us to be mindful that our way to God is only one among many others. In the end, actually, each person finds his or her own method—variations perhaps of one of the main schools, but his own method, because each of us is absolutely unique and has a unique relationship with God.

In his Rule as he lays out the daily program, Saint Benedict allots rather large portions of time to *lectio*. The literal translation of this word is "reading," but in the monastic tradition it connotes much more. It refers to a whole method or way of spirituality which has often been summed up in the four Latin words: *lectio, meditatio, oratio, contemplatio*. This is the method which Father de Mello sets forth.

There is near our monastery two other monastic communities: the ashram of Swami Satchetananda and the Insight Meditation Center, a Theravada Buddhist community. Frequently young people, making the rounds, after visiting these neighbors will come to us. They will have experienced a bit of the eight limbs of yoga with the Hindus and some sitting with the Buddhists. Now they want to experience our thing. They ask: What is your method? I usually answer, the whole of our monastic life is our method. It is hearing the Word of God and keeping it. Whether we eat or drink or do anything else we seek to do all for the glory of God. But if they press me, as they usually do, for something more specific, I say that *lectio divina* is at the heart of our method; then I seek to teach them how to hear the Word of God, meditate upon it, and respond to it in prayer, rest in it in contemplation.

While it is probably true that Benedict's monks, like Basil's before him, were expected to learn to read, the ability to read was not a common attainment in Benedict's time, or for long after. He received into the monastery some rather rough characters, those who understood a beating better than wise counsel. Their reading ability may have been minimal. *Lectio* for Benedict and the early tradition had a broader connotation than simply reading. It meant receiving the revelation of God's love.

The place par excellence to receive this is, of course, the Sacred Scriptures. "I call you no longer servants but friends because I make known to you all that the Father has made known to me." In the Scriptures God reveals himself most intimately. The early monks often memorized large portions of these. Even when I entered the novitiate thirty years ago, we were expected to know many psalms and readings by heart. For the monk, *lectio* might be calling up these texts from memory. It might be hearing another read. Frescoes, icons, and later stained glass could be a source for *lectio*. Eastern Christian monks frequently stand before the holy icons and listen to them. In the Middle Ages the whole of the Scriptures found their way into stained glass. Today cassettes offer us a wonderful means whereby others can in a very living way share faith with us and open the Revelation, or simply read the Scriptures to us while we walk, run, drive, eat, bathe, shave, rest, or work.

There are different kinds of sacred reading. We read to know—sacred study. It is important that we keep up our sacred study and keep our faith culture abreast with our secular culture. We read to act—spiritual reading; it is meant to motivate us, to influence the will. And there is *lectio*; it is meant to bring us into immediate communication with God.

God speaks to us most intimately through the revelation, whether it reaches us in word or art form or through the faith experience and commentary of his saints. As I write this I look out upon a magnificent seascape. A strong wind moves the grasses to bow repeatedly to their Lord. The vast horizons tell of his expansiveness. The cries of the gulls echo our common cry to God. He who is invites to an ever fuller share in his beauty. He lets his creation speak of himself and carry us beyond itself to him. For *lectio*, all creation is a book that speaks of God, and that is what we long to hear.

We hear the word and we want it to come alive in us to form us. The image may rest in our mind's eye and we enter ever more fully into it. Or the word may repeat itself again and again—not necessarily on the lips, though it might, but at least in the mind till it forms the heart. Early monastic meditation did not rely on a lot of thinking, on elaborated technique, as did the later schools. The process was more passive, allowing the revelation to form us and call us forth. This is *meditatio*.

The response to this is *oratio*, prayer. God's revelation can call us forth to many different responses. At times repentance is strong—our response has in sum been so poor. Thanksgiving rises up—to a God so patient, so good, so generous, so loving. There is petition—we sense our needs. But ultimately it is love longing for communion. And when this final disposition takes full hold of us it is *contemplatio*.

These are not so many stages along the way. It is true, at certain points in our life one or the other will prevail, and our constant tendency is toward the union of contemplation. But each day has its grace. One day we seem to read a lot, and nothing seems to call us forth. Another day we are as it were possessed by a word that repeats itself constantly. Some days we sense all reading and thinking as so much distraction; we simply want to rest in the Lord. A method like Centering Prayer can help us here.

As I have said, Saint Benedict allotted generous portions of the day to *lectio*. He was legislating for monks. A later writer, the author of the *Cloud of Unknowing*, undoubtedly a monk, writing for lay persons, spoke of periods of the day to be set aside. Most traditions have recommended two periods a day: one in the morning, another in the evening, at those cardinal points of sunrise and sunset—the empowering of a day's activity, the completing of a day's activity.

Most any text can be used for *lectio*. It is better if it is a text we are familiar with. Then we are not pushed on by curiosity to see what comes next. The Scriptures are by far the best text. Each will find the passages that best speak to him or her. For me it has always been the Last Supper discourse: John 14–16.

When we come to *lectio* the most important thing is our desire. The Lord will reveal himself and enter into our lives to the extent we believe this is really possible and want it. "Ask and you shall receive, seek and you shall find." No one respects our freedom as completely as he does. "Behold I stand at the door and knock and *if* one opens I will come in." He never pushes the door open. He waits for us to open. This is what we do in our *lectio*— we open the door of our mind and heart for him to enter. And he will. If not precisely and experientially at the time of our *lectio*, then some other time, at a time perhaps when we least expect it but most need it. He has made us to be happy with him through an intimate union of love. He wants this even more than we do. He never lets our invitation go unanswered. He comes.

It is important to begin our *lectio* with an ardent plea to the Holy Spirit. "Eye has not seen, nor ear heard, nor has it entered into the heart of man what God has prepared for those who love him, but the Holy Spirit makes it known to us." "I will send the Holy Spirit, the Paraclete, who will abide with you. He will make known to you all that I have revealed to you." It is the Holy Spirit who inspired the Scriptures and the Fathers who have written on them out of their deep love and experience. It is he who dwells in us and will make them come alive in us. We depend upon him and should begin our *lectio* with a fervent prayer to him.

We may in our *lectio* just simply read and let the text speak to us as it will. We might even let the words quietly wash over us as we abide in our longing for God. Or we might more actively challenge the Lord and ourselves in the communication. Do we hear the Lord speaking in the second person or the third? Is he speaking directly to us or in general? Saint Augustine said of the Psalms that they are speaking to us about Christ, or Christ speaking to the Father, or we speaking to Christ. The Gospels and all Scripture can be taken in these ways, and others; especially can they be Christ speaking to us calling forth our response. But we want to guard here the difference between *lectio* and that spiritual reading which is aimed at motivating our life. In the case of the latter we do want to enter into a reflective process. We might ask ourselves such questions as:

Which person am I in the scene? Why?

What is so important about this event? Where does this fit into all Jesus came to accomplish?

Is there anything about Jesus here which especially draws me?

Is there any way he would like me to carry on the work I see him doing here?

Is there anything here which tells me how I could be more like him in the way I look at life and people?

What has this to do with Church or society, with my family, community, friends?

Does it make a difference?

Hearing the Scriptures this way can be very exciting and it can change our lives. We do need to make time for this kind of spiritual reading. But this is not precisely what *lectio* is about. *Lectio*, properly speaking, does not seek information or motivation, it seeks communion and union. We are with the Lord and he speaks to us in our own language.

Recently I received two different renditions of Psalm Twenty-three. The first was from a young man who had been a hippie and wanted to share with me how he saw things in his hippie days:

> The Man upstairs is the sheep-keeper;
> I am with it.
> He makes me sack out on the lawn.
> He leads me by the quiet pond, and peps up the inner man.
> He leads me down the straight and narrow to keep his name clean.
> Even though I stroll through the graveyard scene,
> He doesn't bug me,
> For we're in it together and your hot rod and your stick,
> They're the most.
> You spread the cloth before me even in Squaresville.
> You plaster the dandruff, my mug spills.
> Yea, man, the most and the best shall dog me till the daisies sprout,
> And I shall roost in Endsville till chickens lay square eggs.

More attractive is this from a Japanese friend:

> The Lord is my pace-setter, I shall not rush.
> He makes me stop and rest for quiet intervals;
> He provides me with images of stillness, which restore
>   my serenity.
> He leads me in ways of efficiency through calmness of
>   mind,
> And his guidance is peace.
> Even though I have a great many things to accom-
>   plish each day
> I will not fret, for his Presence is here.
> His timelessness, his all-importance will keep me in
>   balance.
> He prepares refreshment and renewal in the midst of
>   my activity
> By anointing my mind with his oils of tranquillity.
> My cup of joyous energy overflows.
> Surely harmony and effectiveness shall be the fruit of
>   my hours
> For I shall walk in the pace of my Lord and dwell in
>   his house forever.

It is the tradition, as I have stated, to devote some time regularly in the morning and evening to prayer. In a gracious space the Word is more welcome to find the time to unfold its mystery and lead us into the full contemplative experience. We are incarnate persons, so time and place are important. I have already spoken of this. Besides these special times with our Beloved, we can take moments in the day to let him say a word to us. A small pocket Bible or New Testament will allow us to receive a word while we wait in line in the bank or stop at a red light. In one Christian tradition, I found the practice of the "bed Bible." When we are retiring, we take up the Bible, read a verse, and place the Bible on our shoes. As we fall asleep we meditate on the verse received. In the morning as we take the Bible from our shoes and place it back on the pillow we read another verse which we carry through the day. This is *lectio* well integrated into lay life.

The Benedictine method is very simple and one that is most proper for the Christian. As Christians we are sons and daughters of the Book. It is our privilege to have received the Revelation. God has spoken to us. Most properly, then, is our prayer one of listening to God speaking to us and responding to that. Other methods may begin with our activity. For us all prayer, our very being, is a response to one who has first spoken to us in the creation—our own creation—and the Revelation. All that we are is a response to his creative love. Using the Benedictine method we make our times of prayer moments that fully embrace the reality, moments that fill us with great peace and joy. If you have practiced it you know what I am talking about. If you have not, try it and you will soon know the experience. Listen and know that he is God, the God who loves you so, who loves you with an everlasting love and has prepared a place for you in his Kingdom.

The Opus of God

I entered the monastery thirty-one years ago. I remember well meeting Father Paul, the novice master. A brilliant man, a professor at Amherst before he donned the monastic habit, he had deeply sunken eyes that seemed to burn and sparkle. There was often a mirth in his caring love. He seemed to see through our notiviate confusions and bespeak assurance that it would all come out all right. He is well in his eighties now and still going strong, the same light and mirth in his eyes.

As he probed me that day and in the weeks and months that followed, he was gently but incisively exploring to see if I was truly seeking God, if I was growing in zeal for humility (I had a long way to go—and still do), for obedience, and for the *opus* of God. For this is what Saint Benedict says the novice master should do.

To truly seek God—this is the very essence of monastic life; indeed of all Christian and Jewish life by precept and all human life by the very exigency of nature: Love the Lord your God with your whole mind, your whole heart, your whole soul, and all your strength. This is first. Monastic life means making this *the* thing of one's life. For the monk, the Lord is the love of his life. This is why we must be celibate—so that we can freely center all our being and love in God and with him share his concerned love for every one of his children, our brothers and sisters.

Concretely for the sons and daughters of Saint Benedict this allness to God expresses itself in three interrelated concerns. We must be humble, setting aside our own ambitions, so that we can be a complete "yes" to God. We must be obedient, so that our whole being may be fully integrated into the divine plan. The passion of our lives must be that the *opus* of God, his wonderful creation, his masterpiece, might attain its ultimate meaning: to truly glorify its munificent and most loving Creator.

Often *Opus Dei* is taken to mean the Divine Office, the services of praise monks and nuns celebrate in choir. Indeed, Saint Benedict does take it in this sense and this may be the primary sense for him. But these Offices have their meaning only because they are the key moments when the monk or nun lays aside all other activity to fulfill most solemnly his or her role as the high priest of creation, giving voice and heart to the rest of creation to praise its Maker. It is the moment when most precisely the *opus* of God seeks to reflect back the glory of its Creator. It is at the Office, in the liturgy, that the creation attains its summit, its focal point.

Not only the monastic, of course, is called to this. Every Christian who has been baptized into Christ shares in his priesthood, the High Priest of all creation. Every Christian is called to enter into his ultimate act of love and give to the rest of creation a divinized mind and heart with which to glorify the Maker. We need to let all the beauty, all the reality of God's creation enter into our hearts and then enfold it in our love so that it may ascend to him with that love. The *Opus Dei*, the Divine Office, seeks to give voice to that ascension and effect it in and through us. The hours in choir are the high point of the monk's day but they are or should be and will be the high points only if they are the expression of the basic attitude and activity of his whole day and life. His whole being is to be a "Glory be to the Father, to the Son, and to the Holy Spirit."

Some years ago a controversy raged concerning the primacy of liturgy or of contemplation. There were eminent theologians on both sides of the issue. Happily it petered out and these men of learning went on to devote their time and talents to better ends. In fact, liturgy and contemplation are both expressions of the same basic attitude and movement of the spirit.

"Contemplation" is an interesting word. It comes from Latin derivatives. "Con" means "being with": *confraternity*—being with the *fratres*, the brothers; *communion*—being in union with. "Tion" implies an abiding state of "being with." Being with what? The *templa*: When the priests of ancient Rome sought to know the will of the gods, they searched the heavens; in particular they watched the flight of birds through a particular segment of the skies known as the *templa*. In time, the *templa* was projected on earth to become the *templum*, the temple, where people came to know the will of the gods, to enter into union with them. "Contemplation" is a state of being with the will of God, the movement of God, of being with God Himself.

The liturgy is a school where through sign and symbol, word and music, our minds and hearts are formed to be in union with the movement of God, with God Himself.

The basic unit of the liturgy is the day. In the Jewish tradition it begins at evening. Early the Christian communities separated from the evening prayer of Vespers, or the service of thanksgiving, another office which they called Compline, the completing service. It marked a completion: "Now let your servant depart in peace, O Lord." It is a dying. "Lord, grant us a peaceful night and a perfect death." It is a dying so that we may rise again. We go down into the tomb so that we may share more fully in Christ's resurrection as the Son rises with the sun. The going down into the waters of baptism and rising out of them with Christ is renewed as the abbot sprinkles each monk with blessed water and sends him off to his cell. The monk will die to this world as he falls to sleep. He may more radically die to this world as he watches in the night and is stripped of all consolation save the hope of the coming of the Risen Christ at dawn. (This is developed more fully in an earlier chapter in this book.)

In the aftermath of the Second Vatican Council, liturgists sought to suppress Compline as a "later" innovation and a redundancy of Vespers. Two evening offices are not necessary, they said. At first the monks docilely accepted this, but within a short time, in almost every monastery the Office of Compline returned. A deeper instinct prevailed. A basic element of Christian liturgy is this daily dying and rising with Christ; we need a completing Office.

These are the basic Offices: Vespers—Compline, and Lauds, the rising with Christ, the coming of the Risen

Lord into our day, our life. "Blessed be the Lord God of Israel, for he has come to his people . . . the tender mercy of our God who from on high brings the rising Sun to visit us, to give light to those in darkness and the shadow (or image) of death, and to guide our feet into the way of peace." Watching is important for the monk—the Vigils; but this may not be as easily incorporated into your life. The other Hours can more easily be brought in.

You can, of course, use the Office in an approved Book of Hours. These may seem long and complicated. If you cannot pray the whole of an Office, it is enough to pray what you can. You might prefer the Cistercian way. The Cistercians do not have a small office book, only the large books they use in choir. So when they travel they construct their own Office, using the Bible. Each hour is usually composed of a hymn, psalm(s), reading, and prayer which may be quite spontaneous, flowing from reflecting on the reading.

A brief service of thanksgiving can perhaps be connected with your evening meal—before or after. This can easily make it a family or household celebration. A Compline prayer before retiring can be a most intimate moment of prayer for loved ones together. Light a candle before an image of our Lord and let the specialness of this completion of the day peacefully embrace you. Not much need be said: perhaps a psalm (I like 129/130 or the following or 90/91), a word from Scripture ("You are in our midst, O Lord; your name we bear. Do not forsake us, O Lord, our God."), and an Our Father or some spontaneous prayer, and then, if you will, a salute to Mary, the caring Mother: Hail, Holy Queen.

The morning prayer might be more personal: a morning offering, some inspiring reading, a time of silent meditation. I know a friend who listens to hymns and psalms on his cassette player while he showers and shaves to prepare for the reading and centering that will follow. You might find the chapel of your car a good place to celebrate Lauds and Vespers as you drive to and from work. Jogging provides another possible time and place. Some pray with recorded Offices from the abbey. Each individual, or couple, or household, will find its own way to celebrate the resurrection and enter into the life of a new day with the Risen Lord.

Besides the basic rhythm of the day there is the rhythm of the week and the year. I will say more about the week with its creative labor and Sabbath rest when I speak of work.

The liturgical year invites us to enter into the full flow of salvation history. With the First Sunday of Advent we come out of chaos, look to an ultimate consummation, and enter into the longings of a people for a Savior. When Christ does come at Christmas, we begin to live this central life of human history with him, first in large steps, but as it nears its consummation, day by day, hour by hour in Holy Week till the liturgy comes to a halt on Holy empty Saturday. We need a night watch, a very full liturgy to enter into the Paschal mystery. "This is the night when heaven and earth are joined together." We live the joyful forty days with Christ. We pray with Mary and the Eleven, awaiting the outpouring of the Spirit. We go forth with the Church carrying this whole created project with green hope toward the consummation when all will be

Christ's even as he is God's. One of the liturgical reforms of the Second Vatican Council of which I am especially happy is the recognition of Thanksgiving as a full liturgical feast. As we lay all at the feet of Christ the King our hearts are necessarily filled with thanksgiving.

This re-presentation of salvation history in the liturgical year is not just a calling to mind, a symbolic drama; it is a real "making present." These events, all of them, exist now in God's eternal "now" and the liturgy brings them from his "now" into our time. Christ is really born on Christmas in sacramental mystery. It is a present reality. He lives his life, he dies, he rises, he ascends and sends his Spirit, he lives on in his Church. This is the reality of the people of God, those baptized into Christ. We want to enter fully into it.

Home liturgy can help. The Advent wreath can gather the household on the Sundays of Advent and remind them each day that he is coming; the grace of Christmas, the best of gifts, is something to look forward to. An empty creche can heighten the longing of the last days till he comes. Epiphany can mean gifts to the Christs in our lives. Celebrating his baptism the family can renew its commitment to one another in a renewal of baptismal promises. A household fast, if it be only from dessert on certain days, can make Lent more of a time with Christ in the desert. Each day can have its particular little acts of self-denial with alms for the poor, an offering to be brought to church on Holy Thursday. A Seder meal at home can make the Last Supper Liturgy much more meaningful. Perhaps Jewish friends will grant you the privilege of joining in theirs or help you prepare your own. Each home should have its

Paschal candle lit each time the household gathers for a meal or prayer during these forty days of Resurrection. The Risen Lord is truly in our midst. The ten days till Pentecost could be marked with a daily gathering for special prayers with Mary and the Apostles disposing us to receive more fully the Spirit who will guide us through the days ahead. A sharing of the Sunday readings at supper on Saturday or Sunday could help the household move with the whole people of God through the weeks of summer and fall so that the sense of participation in bringing about the ultimate victory and reign with Christ will be heightened. The liturgical year is our year, our life, but we share its fruit and its hope only to the extent we do make it ours and enter into its movement.

At the heart of all, of course, is the Mass. We tend to see and experience things in a linear fashion, one event succeeding another and passing into history. God dwells in an eternal "now." All that ever was and will be is now present in him. If I were to try to express it in an image I might say that while we see things stretched out in a line he sees them all piled up, one atop another, in a single point of time. And at the top of the heap is the greatest act of all creation, the focal act of all creation.

God is love. We are made to his image and likeness. We are all that we are to be to the extent that we are love, lovers, sharing in the love of God become man's in his Son. The greatest act of creation is the greatest act of love in creation, that act whereby the Son offered the Father the greatest thing in creation, his human life. Greater love than this no man hath than he lay down his life. All our love has its meaning and fullness only to the extent it participates in his supreme act of love.

We can reach beyond time into God's "now" to touch that supreme act at any time by our faith. But God Himself in his tremendous mercy and love has given us a ritual act whereby that supreme act of love is brought into our time and made present whenever a priest places that ritual in memory of his Son. The Mass and Calvary are in no wise distinct. The one supreme act of love, abiding ever in the "now" of God is made present on our table by this ritual act just as truly as it was present on the Cross in the heart of the Son. This is the significance of the Mass, and we are invited to it daily.

If your physical presence is absolutely impeded, then reach out in faith and enter in spirit into the Mass being offered each day in your parish or community and make it yours with Christ in God. In the essential act of the Mass liturgy and contemplation are absolutely one. In the Mass the *opus* of God, his masterpiece, has its ultimate expression. To the extent we enter into the Mass we celebrate the *Opus Dei* and bring the creation to consummation in ourselves to the glory of God the Father in the Son through the Holy Spirit.

The son and daughter of Saint Benedict is to be characterized by his and her zeal for the *Opus Dei*, for the celebration of the liturgy as the summing up and expression of the glorification of God that ascends from the whole of creation. Benedict keeps his monks and nuns close to the movement of the creation. His horarium moves with the hours of the day and the seasons of the year. Monks and nuns know the longer quieter hours of watching of the winter and the more active days of seed time and harvest. They are priests of creation in touch with their flocks. A good ecology, a reverence for life are all part of it. But this is the call of all baptized. We are all baptized into Christ's priesthood, the priesthood of creation. Don't let artificial light and city streets keep you from noticing sunsets and sunrises, from experiencing the spring of new life and the harvest of fall. If you don't have a farm, at least have a window box or a few pots of earth. We are the priests of creation. We are the priests of sinful man. At this moment the prospects of history are bleak and threaten to become ever more bleak. All the more reason why we have to live to the full, in liturgical mystery, the history of salvation. We still sin. Christ still saves. In the end *he will reign.* Whether we must first pass through a cataclysm, a nuclear holocaust or not—different ones interpret the Scriptures differently—in the end *he will reign.* And we with him. And even now, in the liturgy, we are welcome to experience already the ultimate triumph in the reign of Christ our King. Perhaps now more than ever before does zeal for the *opus* of God need to characterize the Christian to bring healing and hope to a world so desperately in need of the presence of the saving Passion of Christ and his ultimate act of love.

The Good of Obedience

There is a classical story that comes from the desert tradition. It is ascribed to many different Fathers. In one version it goes something like this:

> It was said of Abba John the Dwarf that he withdrew and lived in the desert at Scetis with an old man of Thebes. His abba, taking a piece of dry wood, planted it and said to him, "Water it every day with a bottle of water, until it bears fruit." At the end of three years the wood came to life and bore fruit. Then the old man took some of the fruit and carried it to the church, saying to the brethren, "Take and eat the fruit of obedience."

Obedience was held in the highest esteem by these desert fathers and pushed sometimes to very great extremes:

> One of the inhabitants of the Thebaid came to see Abba Siseos one day because he wanted to become a monk. The old man asked him if he had any relations in the world. He replied, "I have a son." The old man said, "Go and throw him in the river, then you can

become a monk." As he went to throw him in, the old man sent a brother in haste to prevent him; "Stop what you are doing." But the other replied, "The abba told me to throw him in." So the other said, "But afterwards he said not to throw him in." So he left his son and went to find the old man and became a monk, tested by obedience.

There is, of course, something of a biblical precedent for this test, but it is a bit frightening when men act as God. These men had a simplicity that dared such things, for they were of the race of Abraham, men of obedience, and it was for them the great virtue.

Four monks of Scetis, came one day to see the great abba, Pambo. Each one spoke of the virtue of his neighbor. The first fasted a great deal; the second embraced great poverty; the third had acquired great charity; and of the fourth they said he had lived twenty-two years in obedience to a senior. Abba Pambo said, "I tell you the virtue of the last is the greatest. Each of the others has acquired the virtue he sought. But the last one, restraining his own will, does the will of another. Now it is of such men that the martyrs are made, if they persevere to the end."

Abba Rufus expatiated on this at greater length:

He who remains sitting at the feet of his spiritual father receives a greater reward than he who lives alone in the desert. One of the Fathers said, "I have seen four orders in heaven: in the first order is the sick man who gives thanks to God; in the second, the man who observes hospitality and for that reason, gets up to serve; in the third, the man who crosses the desert without seeing anyone; in the fourth, the man who obeys his Father and remains in submission to him for the Lord's sake. The one who was living in submission was wearing a chain of gold and a shield and had greater glory than the others. I said to him who was guiding me, 'Why does the one who is least have more glory than the others?' He answered me, 'He who practises hospitality acts according to his own will; he who lives in the desert goes away of his own free will; but the last one possesses obedience. Having abandoned all his desires, he depends on God and his own Father; it is because of this that he has received more glory than the others.'" See, my child, how good obedience is when it is undertaken for the Lord. You have partly understood the elements of this virtue, my children. O obedience, salvation of the faithful! O obedience, mother of all the virtues! O obedience, discloser of the kingdom! O obedience opening the heavens, and making men to ascend there from earth! O obedience, food of all the saints, whose milk they have sucked, through you they have become perfect! O obedience, companion of the angels!

Amma Syncletica (there were desert mothers, too!) was more succinct: "Obedience is preferable to asceticism." Indeed, Abba Antony the Great said, "Obedience with abstinence gives men power over wild beasts" (the beasts being the strong passions that rage within us). Abba

Hyperachios in the end indicates why obedience is held in such high regard:

> Obedience is the best ornament of the monk. He who has acquired it will be heard by God, and he will stand beside the Crucified with confidence for the Crucified Lord became obedient unto death.

In a word (according to Abba Isidore), "In obeying the truth, man surpasses everything else, for he is the image and likeness of God."

Saint Benedict is then very much in line with tradition when he begins his *Rule for Monasteries.*

> Listen carefully, my son, to the master's instructions, and attend to them with the ear of your heart. This is advice from a father who loves you; welcome it, and faithfully put it in practice. The labor of obedience will bring you back to him from whom you had drifted through the sloth of disobedience.

In every human grouping, even if it be only two or three, someone has to be empowered, at least transiently, to make the decisions, or the group will often be paralyzed. The richness of human personalities, the multiplicity of possibilities, make consensus an elusive goal, often difficult if not impossible to attain. And life must go on. So concensus expresses itself in the willingness to choose or accept and obey a leader.

But the obedience of which the Fathers speak is not primarily the functional obedience required by organization, however important this may be to the good order of the monastery and monastic community. The Fathers are concerned with deeper values.

By innate dignity, all human persons are essentially equal. It is below our dignity to obey any other human person simply as a human person. If we do obey a superior or boss in a community or organization, it is because we freely choose to cooperate with the group in attaining its goals. A good of obedience is here—we cooperate as equals with different roles—but not *the* good of obedience.

One alone is to be obeyed ultimately: God in his guiding Spirit. "Eye has not seen, nor ear heard, nor has it entered into the heart of the human person, what God has prepared for those who love him, but the Holy Spirit makes it known to us." We want to know the will, the plan of God, and fully conform ourselves to it. This is the only way to happiness. God made us to be happy with him.

Recently I received one of those new watches with a number of buttons on each side. When I push one it lights up, when I push another I get the date, a third will turn it into a stopwatch, and so on. Fortunately for me, there was a booklet with the watch which explained it all: if I push the third button twice I reset the alarm, and so forth. If I cavalierly threw away the booklet, I might have eventually figured it all out—*might*, and after a long time. The human person with his infinite potential is the most enriched being in God's creation. The Lord has given us means of knowing how to attain our purpose, how to function well and be happy. This involves obeying him, his Scriptures (his rule book), and his Church (the guide who helps us interpret his rule book). All too many of us cavalierly throw the rule book away, or leave it unread, and ignore his Church. Even those of us who do accept these find it difficult to be constant in our response to them. We have lots of ideas of our own.

So, the monk or nun enters a "school of the Lord's service." By committing ourselves to obey a superior and making such obedience a part of our daily practice, we hope to learn how better to obey the Lord. More practiced in setting aside our own will, we can more readily do it to conform to the Divine Will.

But there is more to monastic obedience than this. It is not always easy to discern the will of God in all the details of life. By entrusting our way to a *pneumaticos*, a spirit-filled *alba* or *amma*, we can benefit by the discernment of one who is more under the influence of the Spirit than ourselves. In the later institutionalization of the monastic orders there has been added to this the gift which Christ gave to his Church to guide: "He who hears you, hears me." Nonetheless, Saint Bernard constantly exhorted his monks to pray most earnestly that he would be guided by the Spirit in serving them. It is the faith of the disciples which guarantees that God will not let them down in the guidance they receive from their superior.

One of the benefits of this obedience is freedom. The monk walking in the way of obedience is freed from having to devote time and energy to discerning God's will in so many of the details of life. He can simply do what he is told and walk with God. This could, of course, be a disguise for laziness or undue dependency. It is only the mature who can truly obey, like Christ. The dependent go

with the flow for less than fully human reasons, rather than
seek maturely to embrace the will of God. The immature
struggling for a sense of self cannot obey for they fear that
in subordinating themselves to another they will lose themselves. Mature persons can submit themselves freely to another without fear of losing themselves. They rather see
obedience as the way to more surely attain what they want.

There is yet another important dimension to obedience,
beyond the ascetical. In vowing obedience as monks or
nuns we place ourselves wholly at the disposal of the
Church: the local Church (our community) and the
Church universal. We become gifts. We are to lay down
our lives for our brethren and friends. In our lifetime commitment we seek to be one with our Master who was obedient unto death. Obedience is the fulfillment of dis-
cipleship. But for the Christian it is more. We have been
baptized into Christ, made profoundly one with him. To
be fully who we are we must, like him, seek always to do
the things that please the Father. This is the summit of
Christian obedience. "He who loves me, keeps my commandments." It is the expression of love that wants to be
wholly one with the Beloved. If as monks or nuns we open
ourselves to allowing even the least details of our lives to
be regulated, it is because we want to be totally conformed
to the will of God, our Beloved. I exist not to do my own
will, but the will of him who created me. Thy will be
done.

The average lay person has plenty of opportunities to
obey. The red lights and the stop signs, speed limits and
traffic cops. We can obey out of fear of the consequences
or out of consideration of others and good order. But we

can go beyond this and see even in these details of life an opportunity to come into harmony with the will of God, to express our love for him. Saint Paul reminds us: All government comes from God, the civil authorities were appointed by God. And Saint Peter: For the sake of the Lord, accept the authority of every social institution . . . God wants you to be good citizens. There is the obedience due to the Church which touches so many details of life if we are listening. There is the obedience that makes things flow smoothly and efficiently at the office or shop. There is the obedience in the home.

True obedience doesn't involve just doing what we are told. There can be a call to blind obedience but there is great danger that such obedience will be infantile. True obedience involves a responsibility to help the superior or leader in discernment. We do not want blind authority. We want to help authority to discern. The superior, too, must be a person of obedience, listening to what God is saying through those he is called to lead—as Saint Benedict says: The Spirit sometimes speaks through the juniors— and we must be obedient to that.

Saint Benedict has a most curious chapter in his Rule: What we are to do if the superior assigns an impossible task. The Holy Father says the monk is to choose an appropriate time and patiently explain his inability to his superior. But if the superior insists, he must in love obey. In so doing we sometimes find our judgment was off, influenced by our passions perhaps. Or we find God coming to our assistance and supplying for our limitations. However, in the event we may find the task is actually impossible, God teaches us, our superiors, and others, through our failures.

If there is one instance in the Rule when the loving and benign Father of Monte Cassino speaks with vehemence, it is when he condemns the vice of murmuring. As we perceive the good of obedience, we can see why he does. If the heart of obedience is a quest to be a complete "yes" to God in love, murmuring is diametrically opposed to this. Obedience with murmuring is a charade. It is obedience motivated by some intention not worthy of the human person. It is to miss the whole point of obedience.

Another precious school of obedience a lay person can choose is that found in a relationship with a spiritual father or mother. In the Eastern or Byzantine Christian tradition this practice remains fully alive. The renewal of the Sacrament of Reconciliation in our Western tradition is a good step in this direction. The reconciliation room offers the opportunity to sit down and have a good, sincere, open talk on a regular basis with a spiritual father. If we come with faith and confidence we can depend on God to speak to us through him. Oftentimes it is only when we talk something out openly and frankly with another person that we hear clearly what the Holy Spirit—the only true director of the human spirit—is saying within us.

Saul of Tarsus was riding high as he approached the gates of Damascus. He thought he knew well the will of God. He was sincerely seeking to carry it out. God would not let such sincerity down. He threw Saul down from his high horse and spoke to him. But he did not will to reveal all to him directly: "Go to Ananias." God can and does speak to us directly in the depths of our hearts, but his ordinary way of making his will known to us is through the Church, through a spiritual father or mother. If we truly want to be guided by the creative will of God which is wholly ordered to the glory of God in our happiness and fulfillment, we will want to use all the means we can to assure that we are clearly hearing it and empowered to live it.

The good of obedience, which Saint Benedict and the whole monastic tradition so highly extolls, is perhaps a value little appreciated in our times. A false sense of the democratic spirit does not appreciate it. But if we reflect on its values, we soon become eager to embrace it. This is not to deny that it is a difficult path to follow. Our Master sweated blood and begged to be let off even though it was the most profound aspiration of his life and was the way that would lead to glory:

> Let this mind be in you which is in Christ Jesus. Although he is equal to God in all things he emptied himself becoming obedient, obedient unto death. Wherefore, God has highly exalted him and has given him a name above every other name.

Obedience pertains to the essence of the Christian life.

Like Our Fathers and the Apostles

Saint Benedict certainly held labor in high regard: "When they live by the labor of their hands, like our Fathers and the Apostles, then they are truly monks." He could have chosen yet an even more sublime model: the Lord Jesus himself. For the short time he spent on this earth the greater part of it was spent as a laborer, planing wood and fitting it, delivering orders and bringing in supplies. Later he would choose largely laborers to form his chosen band, though "white collar" workers were not left out. Paul, that apostle-come-lately, though a well-educated rabbi, prided himself on living by the labor of his own hands. The Fathers of Egypt were known to weave and unweave baskets to keep busy but, more practically, they also raised grain and sent it down the river to the poor of Alexandria.

Work is the primal penance imposed upon man by God: By the sweat of your brow you will earn your bread. His Son and his Son's followers have embraced this penance. It is a basic part of Christian asceticism, far more healthy and productive than any of the extras: hairshirts, disciplines, or whatever else. The Father of Western

monks has nothing to say for the feats of the desert ascet-
ics. In fact, he does not even develop the idea of work as
penance. He is more concerned about his monks being
kept busy so they won't be the idle playthings of the evil
one: Idleness is the enemy of the soul. Indeed, Saint
Benedict, far from emphasizing the penitential aspect of
work shows himself a solicitous father. The weak are to
have work to keep them busy but not such that would
overwhelm them or drive them away. They are to have
help so they may serve without distress. The monks are to
be suitably wined and dined so they can work without
grumbling or distress. Indeed all work is to be done in
moderation with consideration for the fainthearted. This
hardly sounds like a penitential regime.

Saint Benedict's thrust lies in another direction. He does
not actually develop his theology of work. He sends his disciples to Saint Basil for it as for other aspects of monastic
spirituality. The great monastic Father of Eastern Christians does write at length about this aspect of the monk's
life.

Saint Basil's teaching on work is contained substantially
in six chapters or the responses to six questions in his
longer Rules. The first, Question 37, lays the solid theolog-
ical foundations for his teaching on work. Much of it is ap-
plicable to all Christians, based as it is on the teaching of
the Sacred Scriptures, yet it has specifically monastic dimensions, placing the monk's work squarely in the context
of his life of prayer. The following chapters display Basil's
practicality and wisdom, and address themselves more
specifically to the monastic: the sort of work suitable for a
monk, how he should act in the business world (Questions

38–40). His final question (42) on the dispositions of the laborer can be readily applied to any Christian life, as can much of the preceding chapter (41) which, nonetheless, underlines what is the primary virtue and concern of monastic labor—obedience.

Obedience to the superior and community in this matter of one's work is absolutely fundamental for Saint Basil, yet this is ultimately only a concrete expression of one's obedience to God's will as expressed in the Scriptures. In the course of these six chapters we find forty-four Scripture quotations.

The Saint's exegesis is sometimes surprising. His main base is no particular text but the example of Christ. And that is as it should be for all who call themselves Christians, his followers, and for the monks who are to find their primary spiritual father in this Father of the World to Come. Saint Paul is also a model, he who so forcefully proclaimed himself a spiritual father, because he is such a wholehearted follower and imitator of Christ our Master.

Although Saint Basil does not neglect the important ascetical and penitential aspects of work—for him it involves struggle and great endeavor, fostering the growth of patience and bringing the body into subjection—he nowhere in these chapters alludes to the primal text of Genesis: "By the sweat of your brow you will earn your bread." Rather, when he comes to speak of the aims and dispositions that should motivate the Christian and monk in his labor, he downplays this role of earning one's own bread. Paul's classic text: ". . . working they would eat their own bread," Basil insists is directed toward the unruly. And in their case, to work for their own food is better than their general uselessness; at least, they will not be a burden to others. The emphasis for this very community-minded Father is on the other. Paul prided himself on his own manual labor in that it freed him from being a burden to others. We are not to seek our own—"Be not solicitous for your life, what you shall eat, nor for your body, what you shall put on." The Christian works that he might have to give to others, for the other is Christ. To trust in one's own work, or even in that of others of the brotherhood, is forbidden. Basil does not forbid monks to work to support themselves—he expects them to do it—but in their labors they are to seek to earn, not to make themselves comfortable, but to keep themselves from being a burden to others and to have something to help others. All selfishness and self-reliance is set aside. Depending on the Lord, the Christian works for him, in himself, and in those with whom he identifies himself.

The Apostle's command "to pray without ceasing" and the monk's communal responsibility to gather repeatedly for prayer are not to be used as excuses for holding back from work. Monks, Christians, are to pray while they work. As he expands on this, Saint Basil gives us some of the most precious teaching to be found in these chapters.

First of all the Saint is very realistic. Sometimes the monks can pray and recite psalms while they work. Saint Pachomius, with whom Basil was surely familiar, made elaborate provisions for this. But Basil recognizes that sometimes this is not possible, or it is not conducive to edification. It would be forced. In such circumstances the monk could at least seek to praise God in his heart with psalms, hymns, and spiritual canticles. Yet he goes further.

Conscious of how God is at every moment truly present in his creative love, bringing forth all that is, Basil notes that we can praise God by being in touch with the reality that it is God who is at each moment of our labor (as I write this chapter and as you read it) giving to our hands the strength to do the task and to our minds the knowledge and insight to inspire and direct it. Furthermore, it is he, present and active, who is providing the materials—keeping also them in being in his creative love—that we are using: both the instruments (the pen in my hand, the chisel or shovel or computer in my brother's) and the matter (my paper, his wood, or earth, or ticker tape). The fully responsive use of these, of our own activity, and the ordination of it all to "the good pleasure of God," is the practical way in which we do pray constantly.

Obedience to the Lord, a constant attentiveness to his presence in all, in the full responsiveness of obedience, this is fundamental in Saint Basil's attitude toward work. Given this, the other attitudes he would have enliven this obedience—the labor of the monk—are not surprising. The monk is to go to his work with enthusiasm, a ready zeal, and yet he is to give it careful attention. He is to strive to work blamelessly because he knows that his true, ever-present overseer is none other than the Lord himself.

This is the simplicity we see prevailing in Saint Basil, and indeed it is an essential quality of monastic life. The monk is one whose eyes are set on the Lord. Saint Basil's simplicity is reflected here in another way. He counsels the laborer to set himself with constancy to one task. "We are incapable by nature of following successfully a number of pursuits at the same time; to finish one task with diligent care is more beneficial than to undertake many . . ." But as always, Saint Basil's moderation prevails. If necessity requires it and one has the ability, he can lend his brother a hand. The Saint encourages this with the concrete and meaningful analogy of the body: ". . . just as, in the case of our bodily members, we support ourselves with the hand when the foot is limping."

A monk wants to live a recollected life, one that is in constant attendance on the Lord. Therefore, in choosing his work he will seek that which allows him a tranquil and undisturbed life, a livelihood marked with simplicity and frugality. It will be an employment for which he will be able to get the necessary materials and tools without great difficulty, sell the products readily, and will not have to get involved in unsuitable or harmful relations. His product will not pamper the foolish and harmful desires of men. Basil suggests such crafts as weaving, shoemaking, construction, carpentry, and metal work. He illustrates his last point from these trades. The weaver should make things that will serve daily life and not fancy things to trap and ensnare a buyer. The shoemaker should seek to satisfy real needs.

Basically, Basil opposes traveling, or anything else that can weaken or rupture the unity among the brethren. He does want men to use their talents, but only in the context of the blessing of the community. Saint Benedict was also strong on this. For Saint Basil, community, unity in fraternity, is of primal import. But Christian community can only be founded on obedience, obedience to the Gospels, to God, and to the legitimate authority, the expression of God's direction, at the center of the community.

Saint Benedict only hints at the richness of Saint Basil's theology in a very telling sentence: all the tools and goods of the monastery are to be looked upon as if they were the vessels of the altar. The monk in his labor is celebrating a liturgy, the liturgy of the creation. Through the sentiments of his mind and heart the things he works with are lifted up to glorify God in a way that is worthy of him. They enter into a free, rational, and loving worship. The monk as he works is to be conscious of his duty to cooperate with the Divine creative energies in moving the creation along towards its goal not only through inducing new material and spiritual forms but in ordering all to the glory of the Father.

This is, of course, not the prerogative of monks, but the call of all Christians. Each task, no matter how humdrum, be it mowing the lawn or keeping the accounts, or any other work, moves the creative project forward. If it is done with love, it brings it to consummation.

We are called to constant watchfulness and prayer: "Pray without ceasing." Work has been seen by some as the greatest obstacle to this. Some monks have even used this as an excuse not to work. Saint Pachomius, the Father of Cenobitism, sought to remedy this by assigning many prayers to be recited while the monks carried out their tasks. There was a whole liturgy for the bakers, prayers for each step in the making of the bread. This was carried to excess with the Cluniac monks. Saint Peter Damian tells rather humorously how the monks said so many prayers going to and from work and preparing for work that there was scarcely any time for the actual work. As we have seen, Saint Basil took another tack, a more intrinsic one. He

would have his monks be aware that what they were working with was an immediate gift from God to them, that
the tools they were using were his gift, and indeed the very
energies with which they labored, that flowed through
their minds and bodies were his immediate activity in
them. Thus all work is prayer, an immediate communion
with God in his creative activity. It is saying in deed,
which speaks much louder and more convincingly than
word: "Thy will be done."

Thus we see there are many aspects to monastic labor: it
is penance, an opportunity to make reparation for our sins;
it frees us from idleness; it offers us an opportunity to serve
others either immediately or through giving alms; it is
prayer; it is collaborating with God in bringing his creation
to its consummation; it is a call to glorify the Maker of all.
Undoubtedly some forms of work seem to fall more into
one aspect and others into another. Our own attitudes will
incline us habitually or occasionally to emphasize one or
another of these dimensions. The important thing is not to
fall into a shallow or materialistic outlook where work is
just work or takes on only its own materialistic ends. Such
work is not worthy of those who are made in the image of
God Himself. We do have to make a living. Jobs do need
to get done. Works of art have their own intrinsic beauty.
Ordering our work to higher goals will not detract from all
this. It will only enhance these ends, incorporate them into
the overall thrust of life and augment our dedication to ac-
complishing them, doing the work well, to the best of our
ability.

We make jam and jelly in my monastery. We do it to

help support ourselves, and it does that well. We seek to make the finest jam and jelly on the market, and many do say Trappist Preserves are the best. In taking in hand the fine ingredients we use, fruit of the earth and labor of human hands, through the love of our labor we give them the opportunity to serve people and glorify God in a new, higher way. We are happy that we can bring additional sweetness to the lives of many through our products. It is our joy to be able to send cases of them to the nearby Catholic Worker Home to give joy and nourishment to our less fortunate brothers and sisters. Sometimes, especially as the hot summer days come along or the machinery begins to break down, work in our jelly factory can be very penitential. But in the end, we do all that we do there because we love God and want to glorify him in Christ, our Lord—the same ultimate reason why I write books, Brother Chris mows lawns, Father Placid plays the organ, Father Henry works with the computer, and Father Robert welcomes guests.

You have your work. It will be more meaningful for you, whatever it may be, if you take all the opportunities it affords to serve and give joy to others; if you reverence the things you work with and are conscious that your working with them gives them an opportunity to express themselves at a higher level through your activity and love; if you share some of the fruit of your labor with those less fortunate; if you do all for the love and glory of your heavenly Father, knowing then that your work is part of the transformation of the whole of creation, including especially yourself.

A good way to begin moving in this direction is to begin each day with a morning offering. Pray:

> Jesus, I offer you all my prayer, work, joy, and suffering of this day, for all the intentions of your Sacred Heart, in union with the holy sacrifice of the Mass throughout the world, in reparation for my sins, and for the intentions . . .

Then, as the day progresses, renew this offering as often as you can.

I cannot write about work and not also write about the Sabbath rest. The Lord worked powerfully for six days. He saw that his work was good, very good. And he rested. It is true, the Father works until now. The creation is ever going on. The monk celebrates the *Opus Dei*, the Work of God, every day. There are tasks that must be taken care of every day. But the Genesis account of the Creator's labor and all the details of the Sabbath laws are God's way of making us aware of a profound human need: to stop, step back from our work, and take perspective. It is very true that if we do not do this, very quickly the motives which make our work worthy of us as human persons, Christians, sharers in the Divine Nature, are lost, and work itself begins to own us and set its own goals. There is much more to the Sabbath rest than getting perspective on our work. But this is an important aspect of it. If we do find that our work is encroaching on the time we should be taking for leisure and prayer, it is time to take warning. In these days when technology has so altered the natural rhythm of human life, it is unfortunately not possible for everyone to enjoy the rhythm of a Sabbath week. It is a value you should not readily give up. But if you are forced to, you should make certain that you do establish a rhythm in your life when periodically, according to your need, you do step back from your regular work and take the space necessary to keep it in perspective.

Sabbath space should not be quickly filled with other albeit different activities. Some diversification of activity can be recreative. But we do need space to be, to let our true selves with our deeper aspirations come to the surface. It is in such leisure we can gain perspective and see if our work is what we truly want it to be. Does it have the place in your life you want it to have? Is it motivated in the direction you want it to be motivated? And how about your leisure, do you get what you want to get out of that? Do you really do what you want to do? It takes some real space and quiet to get sufficiently in touch with ourselves to answer these questions to our full satisfaction. Perhaps we avoid leisure and keep on filling our time because we are afraid of negative answers and being confronted with the meaninglessness of much of what we are doing or the ultimate insufficiency of our motivation. If you do not find in your life a good balance of work and Sabbath, then something surely needs to be examined.

When I show guests through the monastery occasionally on a Sunday, they are struck by the stillness. They ask if anyone is really here. The monks love their Sabbath rest. At the same time the guests will comment on how clean everything is, how well the lawns are manicured, how beautiful the vesture is, how good our preserves are, how peaceful is the whole climate of the monastery. In our rest, the fruit of our labor is present to be enjoyed. That is the way it should be. If your work is relentless, if there is not periodically spaces of leisure where you can enjoy the fruit of your labor, then something is wrong. We should do all God wants us to do. But we should not do more than God wants us to do. If we are not finding due Sabbath we are perhaps doing more than he wants, doing things he wants others to do or wants to take care of himself.

As I write this, I am painfully aware that at this time there are all too many who cannot find work or work that will adequately remunerate them so they can establish a balance in their lives. It would be difficult to overestimate how dehumanizing this is, how much it undermines a person's humanity and participative divinity. We are meant to be participating with the Creator in the ongoing work of bringing the creation to completion. What can I say to these brothers and sisters? To those of us who are better off, I think each of us, according to our proper vocation, should do all we can economically, socially, politically, and through prayer, to remedy this situation. To the unemployed or the underemployed, I hesitate to say anything—words come cheap. But faith does come through hearing. Behind all the inhumanity of people and their plain bungling, there abides a loving and provident God. Trust in him can be the source which will enable you to keep going, keep trying, working out your salvation maybe not with the sweat of your brow but the tears of your heart. God help you, and us all.

"You Are . . . Friends"

"He must grow greater, I must grow smaller." Not smaller in the sense of any diminishment of my being or personhood, of what really matters, of who I am, but only in comparison to who he is, only in regard to anything in my person or in my activity that would impede his increase in me, in himself, in all. This is true love, true friendship. The beloved is placed first. His well-being, his growth, his glory is the concern, the desire. Fortunate has defined love as "transcending one's self for the purpose of nurturing . . . another's spiritual growth." I like this definition.

Saint John Baptist is considered a special patron and model for monks. This is brought out in Byzantine monastic churches by the special place he is given on the iconostasis. There is first of all the icon of Christ, the Pantocrator, the Maker of All; then of Mary, the Panaghia, the All-Holy; then that of the particular patron of the monastery, and finally that of the Prodromos, the Forerunner, John the Baptizer. The choice seems logical enough. We think of his life in solitude: "he lived out in the wilderness." We think of his austerity: "John wore a garment of camel-skin." And of his fasting and abstinence: "he lived on locusts and wild honey." We think of his prophetic witness: "Prepare a way for the Lord, make his paths straight." He was indeed "the voice of one crying in the wilderness." He did come "not eating or drinking." We can well see him as a model of these qualities. But the most beautiful and significant description that John gave of himself does not center on one of these. It is rather his description of himself as *friend*. He was "the bridegroom's friend, who stands and listens, is glad when he hears the bridegroom's voice." He did indeed listen. Even when the Bridegroom was still hidden in his Mother's bosom, when both of them were so hidden, he already heard his voice in the voice of his Mother, and he leaped for joy. He listened and was led by his spirit. Elsewhere in this volume I have written about listening. Here I want to speak about friendship. For in his friendship, even more than in all his other qualities—which indeed were all in service of his friendship —John is our model. And in his friendship, the Precursor is also follower, disciple, for his Master and ours is preeminently friend.

On the night before he died, as he poured out his heart and revealed the deepest meaning of his mission and his relation with us, Jesus said to us: "You are my friends . . . I shall not call you servants anymore . . . I call you friends." He expressed his friendship by coming to be with us and abiding with us: "And know that I am with you always; yes, to the end of time." He shares with us all his secrets, "I have made known to you everything I have learnt from my Father." And finally, "A man can have no greater love than to lay down his life for his friends," and this he did for us.

The monk in his choice of celibacy, in saying "yes" to the call, the invitation to embrace the life of a monk, chooses to be a friend of the Friend, to make that friendship the central reality of his life. And he enters a community of friends, a "school of love" in order to learn through friendship how to be a friend—in order to be a friend to the Friend because "whatever you do to the least of my brethren you do to me."

One of the most beautiful pictures of monastic mythology is that of Saints Antony and Paul meeting in the desert. Antony the Father of Monasticism and Paul the Hermit had long striven to live as true monks. They had heard much of each other, had been encouraged and strengthened in their resolve by each other's example and prayer. At length, moved by the Spirit, Antony knew it was time to seek out his friend. In the loving embrace of these two is epitomized the meaning of monastic friendship. The friendships of youth are very beautiful, exciting, full of promise. But in the embrace of two old friends we see the fulfillment of some of our deepest aspirations.

I shall never forget the day Brother Thomas, after years as an oblate, made his solemn vows and was formally received into our community. Age had already slowed him down a good bit and his eyesight was diminished. After all the monks in the choir had gone up to embrace him to welcome him into the bosom of the community, Tom went in search of Brother Alfred. Ninety years young, nearly blind, "Uncle Alf" usually sat quietly in a corner during the services. Brother Tom knew he was there. At his approach, Alfred came out of his corner, and these two beautiful old men, slowed by age, groping as do the blind, came together in the middle of the choir and embraced. Even as I write this, tears run down my cheeks. There were few dry eyes in the choir that day. Paul and Antony were meeting again.

Monastic history is scored by wonderful friendships. My own blessed patron, Basil, had his school chum, Gregory. With youthful excitement they set out together on the monastic quest. Later they were called forth from their monastery to be archbishops. They had their differences at times, but a magnificent eulogy gives witness to the ultimate triumph of friendship. Saint John Cassian had his dear Herman who shared his long search in the desert. There is the beautiful story of brother and sister, Benedict and Scholastica. When the day was not long enough for their sharing, heavenly rains blessed its prolongation through the night. Even death did not separate them as they shared a common tomb. So many monastic friendships could be recalled. Malachy of Ireland had his prayer answered, and died in the arms of Bernard at Clairvaux so that their relics could be mingled in a common grave. Bernard was a man who knew friendship in its fullest. The letters exchanged between him and William of Saint Thierry, his closest friend, are embarrassingly naked, almost passionate. It was at Bernard's direction that Aelred of Rievaulx wrote as the primer of Cistercian life, a *Mirror of Charity*, which powerfully extols the beauty of friendship, warns wisely of its dangers, and finds its consummation in mystic friendship within the Trinity. Let me quote just one of its more beautiful passages:

It is such a great joy to have the consolation of someone's affection—someone to whom we are deeply
united by the bonds of love, someone in whom our
weary spirit may find rest, and to whom we may pour
out our souls . . . someone whose conversation is as
sweet as a song in the tedium of our daily life. He
must be someone whose soul will be to us a refuge to
creep into when the world is altogether too much for
us, someone to whom we can confide all our thoughts.
His spirit will give us the comforting kiss that heals all
the sickness of our preoccupied hearts. He will weep
with us when we are troubled, and rejoice with us
when we are happy; he will always be there to consult
when we are in doubt. We will be so deeply bound to
him in our hearts that even when he is far away, we
shall find him together with us in the spirit, together
and alone. The world will fall asleep around us, we
will find, and our souls will be at rest, embraced in absolute peace. Our two hearts will be quiet together,
united as if they were one, as the grace of the Holy
Spirit flows over us both.

This work of his early years was not enough for Aelred.
He continued it in a lifetime dialogue with his disciples
the fruit of which he shares with us in his book *On Spiritual Friendship*.

In the centuries following Aelred, monasticism, unfortunately, for the most part, lost sight of this precious element
of its heritage. Monks still gathered in communities. Charity was still extolled as the virtue par excellence. But
friendship lost its place and even became suspect. There
were various reasons for this.

One was the drive to get things done. Monks repeatedly became doers; ecclesiastical doers with parishes, missions, shrines, and schools; material doers, too, with buildings and farms, trade and even industries. There was hardly enough time for minimal friendship with God in prayer; no time to relax and be with brothers in that present sharing that creates friendship. Jesus made time to be alone with his disciples: "You must come away to some lonely place all by yourselves and rest for a while." Even though there was a world to be saved there was time and space for friends.

As monasticism moved into the modern era, there was something of "throwing out the baby with the bath." There were failures in regard to friendship, and lamentable lapses. Monks are men, and sinful men at that. Passion can and has overtaken them. Not all monks are necessarily "straight." They have experienced crushes, attachments, the distractions of love too human, and other failures. Aelred had warned of all this. "Friendship is the most dangerous of all our affections." The Fathers who, like this Saint of Rievaulx, extolled monastic friendship were not oblivious of these dangers. But a later age in seeking to get rid of the pollutions pretty much did away with the beautiful reality. "Particular friendship"—and therefore all friendship, for every friend is particular—became suspect and proscribed.

Some have lamented this, but in fact not all that many. Even in these days of relatively enlightened renewal, when most monks have full freedom to develop deep friendships, few do. The rigorous demands of true friendship, the gift of oneself, one's time, one's preferences, the nakedness and honesty, are beyond the price many are willing to pay—those who have not yet experienced what is purchased by such a price. Anyone who has been graced with true friendship knows the cost and knows the worth. And he knows, too, the ridiculousness of the fear that such friendship will undermine community. It is, in truth, only the one who has been honed by true friendship who can give himself in fullness to communal love. True friends are the best community men.

Some years ago when the Jesuits were moving their large isolated theologate in the wheat fields of Kansas to the campus of Saint Louis University, they asked the Menninger Psychiatric Institute in Topeka to help them arrange their new building in a way that would best facilitate true community. Dr. Menninger himself took an interest in the study and approved the report which noted a very significant fact, one my own community and pastoral experience verifies. It said for a person to relate well in general he needs to have in his life one or two intimate friends, a small group of acquaintances with whom he is comfortable, and a larger stable group with which he identifies. Monks readily identify with the community to which they are attached by a solemn vow of stability. The ordinary circumstances of work and study develop comfortable acquaintances. But monastic structures usually fail to provide the time and the places which facilitate the development of intimate friendships. This is another cause of their absence. Aelred's beloved Ivo begged: "that, as often as you visit your sons here, may I be permitted, at least once, to have you all to myself, to disclose to you the deep feelings of my heart without disturbance."

I believe an extremely important part of monastic renewal lies in recovering this dimension of our heritage. If we enter the monastery to live the essence of the Christian life as fully as possible and to find full support for that, then monastic life should indeed be a school of friendship, everything is to support the growth of friendship among the monks and with their Friend who is their Master and supreme Model.

Christian communities are societies of friends as the Quakers have so well and beautifully realized—because we are called to be disciples of the Friend. Indeed, his one new commandment is to love as he has loved. It is not enough then to tolerate our fellows. We must truly love, transcend ourselves to nurture each other's spiritual growth.

The primary Christian community is the home. Here the basic attitude of wanting the other to increase, to grow greater, must be expressed in making time for each other. We affirm the other's worth and desirability by giving him or her priority when we allot our life's time. We have to take care, especially men, that we do not let projects and doings, accomplishment and productivity squeeze out the gracious space of friendship—as monks all too often have done in their communities. Like Christ, we have to make time and share—share the deepest things of our lives, "all that the Father has made known to me." This is what the "ten and ten" of Marriage Encounter is all about. We need to find the structures that will facilitate the time, the space, true sharing in our home community. I am not necessarily speaking of a husband and wife here, but they should be friends par excellence for it is their sublime vocation to sacramentalize for all of us the love of Christ, the Friend, for his Church and the love we the Church should have for him.

It takes a lot of courage to share with another what the Father is saying to us in our deepest conscience. And a bit of humility. But it is a powerful aid to being true to our truest self. And such sharing undercuts some of the deepest roots of our loneliness and our self-depreciation.

We may say there is no one in our home who would want to share with us at this level, no one whom we can so trust. That may be so now. The fact may be no one would want so to trust us. But, in fact, such sharing, such friendship, responds to a deep desire in all of us. Most of us are blocked by fears. True friendship doesn't just happen. We have to make time for it, cultivate it, gradually open ourselves and mutually uncover successive levels, till at last the light of love can shine into the very depths, and we can rejoice in our shared beauty in complete freedom. It takes time. It takes courage, patience, and humility. It takes a conviction that love and friendship are worth it. The full enjoyment of such a relationship may be long in coming, but even with the first stage the fruits are tasted and the hope and promise great.

Friendship doesn't just happen, nor can it be forced; it is a gift—but a gift that must be accepted and cultivated. To *have* a friend, we must *be* a friend. We must turn from looking at faults—something we are strongly programmed to do in this competitive society of ours—to looking at strengths, beauty, gifts, and talents. The faults and weaknesses must be accepted, too, with a loving, concerned, and healing compassion. Our friendship must be treasured, protected, displayed, not easily given away, put in jeopardy, or abused. We have to channel a lot of time and energy into a developing friendship. In this respect it may be initially truncating in regards to the development of other aspects of our lives. But as we call forth our friend we lay the foundation for further empowerment and support. A true friend becomes for us an icon of Christ, a special shrine where we find and love Christ and experience Christ's love for us.

Particular friendship is at the heart of our lives as Christians no matter what our call. It is when we are willing to walk all the way with one particular friend we develop the self-transcending love that enables us to give ourselves in a Christlike love to all. It is in the experience of a deep full rich human love that we begin to get some real insight into the intimacy to which the Lord, our divine Friend, is calling us. "I shall not call you servants anymore . . . I call you friends."

Holy Joy

We all tend to have our favorite Gospel. For the contemplative it is often Saint John's. The transcendence of his Prologue and the deep sharing of the Sacred Heart at the Last Supper speak deeply to my heart. Some are drawn more by the conciseness and actuality of Saint Mark. I have appreciated Saint Matthew's sense of tradition and fulfillment, his Jewishness. Saint Luke is the ladies' man. Women loom large in his account of salvation history. But it is his joy, especially in the first chapter, that has particularly attracted me to him. The angels sing, the shepherds rejoice. Mary proclaims her Magnificat and old Zachary his Benedictus. And Simeon closes his long life in fulfilled song.

Saint Luke undoubtedly belongs to a tradition, a vein of Judaism which, despite the awesomeness of the God of Sinai, has been able to celebrate his holiness in joy, dancing in spirit with Miriam on the banks of the Red Sea and with David before the Ark. Its joy reaches down to our times in the Hasidim who have brought their heritage through the pogroms of Eastern Europe to Brooklyn Heights.

Monika Hellwig recently described the spiritual outlook of the Hasidim:

> The objective of hasidic spirituality is to become aware of God and united to God everywhere and in all things with sustained passionate and joyful self-abandonment. For the Hasidim the presence of God everywhere and in all things was understood literally. Therefore, intimate union with God was to be sought not only in seclusion but in the everyday life of the community.

As I read these lines I thought how well they also describe the monastic spirituality of the Cistercians. Happiness consists in knowing what you want and knowing you have it or are on the way to getting it. Those who truly seek God, who want God, and have the insight of faith and the gifts to perceive his real presence in every one and every thing, always have what they want. They know that the whole world is the place of God, that all is sacred. They are always happy. Their lives express that joy which is a fruit of the Holy Spirit.

The monk who embraces the primal penance of man: "By the sweat of your brow you will earn your bread," and seeks to support himself by daily manual labor, cannot draw a line between his work and his religious practices. He must seek to overcome any separation of the sacred and the profane and be open to the encounter with God in all. Guerric, Abbot of Igny, a chosen disciple of Bernard of Clairvaux, speaking to his monks one Easter morning brought this out. He was commenting on the Gospel passage where the pious women had gone to Jesus' tomb to anoint him, and found it empty. As they returned along the garden path, they came upon him. Guerric reminded his monks how it sometimes happened that they seemed to seek the Lord in vain as they pursued their sacred reading, went to the Office, and prayed at the tomb of the altar. But as they went off down the path toward their appointed work—lo! there was the Lord.

If the monk goes apart from the world, it is to go to the heart of the world. If he is a fringe person it is not because he is on the outer fringe but the inner fringe. His vocation is one of redeeming the world by a recovery of the integrity of Eden, where in communion and union all the divorce between the sacred and the secular is healed. The community of love, embracing all creation, standing in God—this is the ideal of the monastic school of love. Daily practice and a lively hope bring the joy of knowing it as an attainable object that is actually being attained.

Martin Buber has described four basic virtues cultivated by the Hasidim to overcome the separation of the sacred and secular. They are complementary characteristics which balance each other and lead to a complete integrity. They are the characteristic virtues of the Cistercian monastic life. Saint Benedict spoke of them as truly seeking God, zeal for a humble way of life, zeal for obedience, and zeal for the *opus* of God. Buber catalogues them as *kavana* (single-mindedness), *shiflut* (humility), *avada* (service), and *hitlahavut* (the fire of ecstasy).

Single-mindedness which comes from inner devotion and purity of intention sees only one goal in life. People who truly seek God see all "as it were under a single ray of light." "Whether you eat or drink or whatever else you do, do all for the glory of God." All, natural objects, human activities, social structures, all take on a power and unity, all contribute to what the monk seeks and, therefore, to his joy.

The humility we speak of here—true humility—is not a demeaning of self, comparing self with others, striving to evaluate or devaluate self. No. It is rather a realistic grasp and acceptance of the reality that one is part of the whole, a member of the community, of Christ. The wonder of one's being is still part of something, someone so very much greater. And there is a joy that transcends self in this realization.

It can readily be seen how these two virtues complement each other. The single-mindedness, the devotion keeps us from turning in on ourselves. And our freedom from self-absorption enables us to be wholly turned toward the Lord.

Avada, the work of service or the service of work, is the responsive gift of self in obedience to reality. It involves the work of worship, the response to the transcendent reality of God, as well as the work of service, the response to the needs of our brothers and sisters, the needs of a creation that is groaning and in travail as it strives for the fullness of redemption. Whether the service be sublime or most humble, it is all one, seeking to bring about the ascension of all to God in integral harmony.

Complementary to this daily and sometimes laborious service is that experience of God, *hitlahavut*, the going out of self, the "taste and see how good God is," that engenders a joy that seems to belong to another realm. The peak moments of ecstasy will be few and brief, but the memory of them abides, and something deep within us says that all the strivings of life are worthwhile because of them. The joy of these moments continues to flow as a deep, abiding current in our lives, to be called forth through devotion and service.

There are spontaneous eruptions of joy in the lives of all of us. But such an abiding state of joy does not just happen. It has to be cultivated. It is an option. If I may descend to a very prosaic simile, I often say the whole world is made up of two kinds of people: those who look at the doughnut and those who look at the hole. Some prefer to dwell on the emptiness of life, the lacks, what is missing, not realizing that there cannot be a lack, something missing, a hole, if there is not a context, a fullness from which it is missing. We can choose to dwell on the fullness, on being rather than on the lack of being. We can see the glass half full rather than half empty.

I think it is sadly true that in general people are programmed for suffering more than for joy. We seem almost to enjoy talking about our miseries and dwelling on them. There are no doubt abundant causes for sorrow, concern, and grief. But where sin abounds—and all its effects—grace abounds yet more. We can opt to keep our eyes on the presence and activity of grace in our own lives and in the lives of others and accentuate this with all its hope.

Reprogramming may call for effort, a real program on our part. We can begin by smiling more. Every human being rates a smile and infinitely more. And the first person we might smile at each day is the one we greet in the bathroom mirror. We can make a real effort to make pleasant and complimentary comments as often as possible. We all like to be told how good we look. Our smile and compliment will oftentimes evoke a similar response, reinforcing our own new direction. We can make a practice of letting go of unnecessary negative thoughts and feelings (our prayer word—a quick flight to the center, while the thought is allowed to float away—can be used to advantage in this) and cultivating joyful, positive ones. We can take time out to reflect on each person who holds a place in our lives, noticing all the good things in each—and they are many for each is the image of God—then share this with the person involved and others. Again, one of these persons should be that special person called "me." As an exercise we can think of the worst thing that might possibly happen, and then try to see all the positive things that might flow from it. For example, we might think of ourselves getting hit by a car and landing in the hospital. Positively, it might give us time to do some things we have been wanting to do: reading, writing, praying, painting. We will get a good rest. The insurance company may be good to us and we can take a trip we have been wanting. We might make new friends. Old friends will come and spend time with us. We will get our picture in the newspaper and on television. We will get a new car, and so forth. We can spend more time meditating on the positive aspects of our faith: God's great love for us, Christ's saving grace, the heaven that awaits us, and thank God for all this. Thanksgiving is a source of double joy. And sharing all these reflections with another, a friend, will multiply our joy.

An important part of our program will be review and evaluation. We might each evening at our Compline prayer reflect for a moment on the particular practice we are presently concentrating on: How many times today did I smile? How many times did I fail to smile when I could have? How many compliments did I give today? How many opportunities to say a complimentary word did I miss? How often did I harbor unnecessary negative thoughts and feelings? How often did I cultivate and express positive ones? On our monthly retreat we will want to evaluate our program and its degree of success in reprogramming us for joy. It will probably have to be adapted as we make progress in the direction we want to go.

One would wonder why all do not choose to dwell on the fullness. But a little reflection quickly gives some indications. Such fullness demands a response; it calls forth that inner devotion. It makes us realize our own relative position, the attitude of true humility. It calls for service. There is a cost. But when the cost is paid, it will lead us to joy and ecstasy. Some would rather not pay the price. Nothingness, the hole, makes no demands. We can easily feel superior to a hole. Keeping an eye on the lacks in others enables us to live more comfortably with our own— or so we think, as long as we are coming out of comparative thinking. We can find lots of "reasons" for looking at the holes in life: One must be realistic, practical, prudent, etc. And there is some truth in these reasons. But if we don't see the holes in the context of the fullness, these reasons no longer have any validity. And they do deprive us of so much of the joy of life. To have the courage to look at the fullness of reality and let it call us forth is the way to ever greater joy.

God, our beloved Father, has made a tremendously beautiful universe, and he has made it all for us, for our happiness. We have sadly ignored and countered his plan in many, many ways. His healing grace is at work. If it is initially painful to face the wonder of his love and be convicted of our own unresponsiveness, his mercy is not slow in responding to our misery. Even the past misery becomes a source of joy as we experience the soothing of his healing love.

I remember one of the answers I learned by rote back in Our Lady of Angels grade school: God made me to know, love, and serve him in this world and to be happy with him in the next. At this point I think that catechism answer conveys a real heresy, one that has perhaps done more to undermine Christian life than we can estimate. The implication that God's plan reserves happiness for heaven is enough to cause us at least to question his love if not actually to turn against such a Father. God made us to be happy with him not only in the next life but here and now. Saint Paul reminds us that the fruits of a life in the Spirit are love and joy. Surely there will be sorrows on the journey. The true lover is ever more sensitive to the sufferings of others and the injustices of our society. But deep within, a person in tune with God experiences a constant joy. This is the prerogative of the Christian, the one baptized into Christ, who has in baptism received the Spirit as a gift. The important thing is that we give ourselves time and space to enjoy the friendship of God, to experience his love and his care, to let the whole creation reveal to us his love. Let's keep our eyes on the doughnut and the hole will fill with sweetness—and we will have a jelly doughnut!

He Was Tempted

Saint Benedict uses many different images to describe the monk: he is a soldier doing battle for Christ, our true King; he is a student in the school of the Lord's service; he is son and heir in the household of the Paterfamilias; he is a craftsman laboring in the workshop of the enclosure. In the fourth chapter of his Rule, he provides his craftsman with seventy-two tools for the spiritual craft. They include the ten commandments and other counsels from sacred Scripture. They also include much wisdom from the Fathers.

One of these tools is this: As soon as wrongful thoughts come into your heart, dash them against Christ, as against a rock, and disclose them to your spiritual father. Benedict, the true son of Antony, the Desert Father, knows what monsters these evil thoughts can become. Iconography and medieval hagiography have had great fun depicting the temptations of Antony, but they were very real indeed—as every monk comes to experience. So Benedict's advice is quite ruthless. He is undoubtedly thinking of the last verse of Psalm 137: A blessing on him who takes and dashes your little ones against the rock. The rock for us is, of course, as Saint Paul said, Christ our Lord, the source of all grace. As Moses struck the rock in the desert and the people received life-giving water, so too, when we dash our temptations against Christ his grace pours forth to sustain us. As soon as any evil thought arises in our hearts we want to cast it and ourselves at his feet and let the comfort of his love and friendship give us the satisfaction we are tempted to seek elsewhere.

Those who regularly practice Centering Prayer have an excellent tool for handling wrongful thoughts, whether they be actual temptations or just dissipating, useless, or self-deprecating thoughts. With practice, the prayer word gains a great power to bring us to the center, to Christ. In the prayer, we have learned whenever thoughts catch hold of us to use the word to return to the center and let the thoughts flow away. So through the day when unwanted thoughts come upon us, instead of fighting them, which may well strengthen their presence, we can simply with our own prayer word go to the center for a moment and let the unwanted thought or feeling, the temptation, float away.

We are programmed to see temptations as something evil: Lead us not into temptation. It comes as a bit of a surprise then when we read in Saint Matthew's Gospel: "Jesus was led by the Spirit out into the wilderness to be tempted by the devil." This is not quite what we would expect the Holy Spirit to do. Temptation insofar as it is an act of the evil one arising out of his envy and hatred is certainly evil. Insofar as it is the good things of the world enticing our disintegrated nature to act in insubordination, it is not good. But for those who love God, all things work together unto good. The challenge can make us grow, give us fuller insight, make us more like our Lord and Master, who struggled with temptation from the days in the wilderness till he hung naked on the cross and was buffeted with the cry: If you be the Son, come down. Thus Saint James could encourage the first Christians:

> My brothers, you will always have your temptations but, when they come, try to treat them as a happy privilege; you understand that your faith is only put to the test to make you patient, but patience too is to have its practical results so that you will become fully-developed, complete, with nothing missing.

Our Lord had gone into the desert to empty himself as completely as possible of the things of this world in order to be filled with the Spirit, to receive the sure guidance he needed for the mission and ministry that lay head. This is something of the meaning of novitiate in active religious institutes and seminary for diocesan priests, something that is perhaps being missed in our days: the need to go apart and really empty the self to be prepared. It was when Christ had most completely emptied himself, even physically, and was most open to the Spirit that the evil spirit came upon him. We are sometimes surprised to hear of the temptations of holy ones. People sometimes think monks and nuns locked away in their cloisters are free from temptation. Not at all. It was in this the most monastic part of his life that Jesus was tempted. When we take our Christ-life seriously and make true efforts to be like him, the devil becomes more interested in us. When we most open ourselves to the Holy Spirit, the evil spirit, the

deceiver, using the very words of Revelation, seeks to insin-
uate himself.

The devil tried to snare Christ with very literal inter-
pretations of various Scripture texts. Jesus responded with
principles from Scripture. This might warn us to beware of
making too much of individual texts as words from the
Lord; rather always to place them in the context of the
whole Revelation—above all in the context of the two
great commandments.

Christ, our model, faced the onslaughts of the evil one
first in regard to the basic drives of human life: food and
power—control over one's own life and control over others
and the situations of life.

The temptations were very real. Christ was a hungry
man. The sight and smell, the comforting feeling of fresh
bread in his empty stomach quickly arose in his imagination. But not by bread alone does man live, but by every
word that comes forth from the mouth of God. Fasting
does create in us a hunger, a hunger that can be subli-
mated into a deep longing for God and for his Revelation.
The well-fed are often sluggish at their *lectio*. They are
content. There is no incarnation of their spiritual hunger.
There are always vast spaces in our spirit longing for God,
but we can be very much out of touch with them if we are
too intent upon satisfying ourselves on more superficial
levels. Having the courage to deny some of these needs, we
can attend more freely to feeding the spirit. The monk
then does not dwell on his empty tummy but his empty
spirit and lets the hunger he experiences drive him on to a
lectio that is filled with a greater hunger for God.

Monastic life is in many ways very humdrum, very

prosaic. There is an established routine that goes on day after day. The faithful monk's longing for God does grow. There is the temptation to step out of the routine and take some mighty leap in faith, a short cut that will call forth a surge of divine power in this painfully slow work of purification and sanctification. The last words written by the Patriarch of the West, flowing out of years of experience, are these: "Through patience we share in the Passion of Christ"—patience with God, patience with ourselves, patience with everyone else. The temptation to be impatient, to try to force the hand of God is great, the temptation to do things our "brilliant" and "efficient" way rather than letting him work in us through the slowly paced circumstances of daily life and daily fidelity. "You must not tempt the Lord your God." We must let him do it his way and cooperate as best we can, trusting that he will indeed complete the work when it is to be completed and not one moment before. He has everything under control. Sufficient for the day is the evil thereof.

When we have struggled with temptations and by God's grace have been freed from them, we experience a certain spiritual power. It is something of the power that came upon Moses and Elijah, and Christ himself after their fasts and struggles. We should not be too quick to expect this to be a permanent state, nor too surprised if temptations do return. God often gives us seasons of respite before the final struggle. We can enjoy the season of grace but hold it with gentleness and dispossessiveness.

With spiritual power a new temptation can come upon us, the third temptation. All things are ours: All things are yours, and you are Christ's and Christ is God's. But we can become possessive, dominating, judgmental. We have overcome temptation, we have put a restraint on ourselves, our passions, our emotions; why shouldn't everyone else. The Fathers tell this story:

> One day one of the younger brothers was caught in fornication. The elders gathered to judge him and expel him from the community. But Abba Moses did not come. The elders then sent for him, insisting he come. Finally the old man did come, carrying on his back a large basket of sand in which he had poked a hole. The sand trailed out behind him. "Should I come and sit in judgment on a brother when my own sins trail behind me?"

In the litanies we pray: "For peace and compunction all the days of our lives." Compunction, an abiding sorrow for our sins, is a great liberating spirit. It keeps us humbly grateful that we have been freed from our sins. It wards off the temptation to judge others in whom the Lord has not yet brought this about. We accept the Lord God as the sole supreme master of this creation and fully accept his way of working in each of his servants. That he has freed us and works powerfully in us, we rejoice. At the same time we fully accept the limitations of the power he has given us in his Spirit.

This power is especially a power for compassion. Christ is able to be compassionate with us, the Scriptures tell us, because of the things he suffered. So, too, having gone through temptations ourselves, and knowing that we have overcome in the end only by his power, we can have compassion on our brothers and sisters who struggle. We can assure them with Saint Paul: "The temptations you have to bear are no more than people normally have. You can trust God not to let you be tried beyond your strength, and with any trial he will give you a way out of it and the strength to bear it."

There is a very powerful help in overcoming temptation and it is one that monasticism has always held in the highest regard. It is part of the tool Saint Benedict hands his disciple: "And disclose then the temptation to your spiritual father." There are a number of factors that come into play here. First of all, bringing our temptations out into the light fully unmasks them. We see more clearly the deceptions they cloak. Very shame supports us in saying no to them. We are strengthened by the support of our father's prayer, and the knowledge of his prayer and care. We are not alone in facing the enemy of our souls. But there is another element. We should lay before our father all our thoughts and inspirations (especially those we are most tempted to conceal), for sometimes temptation is so subtly presented by the evil one that we can mistake it for a good inspiration. Bringing all to the father, we can receive advice, counsel, and enlightenment.

It is not always easy for a lay person to find a spiritual father or mother, or even a companion for the journey. But if one truly seeks one will find. It is well worth the search and I would strongly urge it. The hope to make real progress in the Christ-life without a guide is almost an illusion. God can, of course, directly and immediately provide all the guidance a person needs. He is not bound to any particular way of doing things. Yet it is his most common way to guide us through others, to have us pilgrims assist each other. We should be slow to conclude it is to be otherwise with ourselves. Rather, we should make every effort to establish a supportive relation with a spiritual father or mother who can walk with us on our way.

Temptation is a part of every Christian life. Monastic tradition gives us a simple response to it: As quickly as possible, as soon as we perceive it, dash it against Christ and let it be exposed to the light. It is not something to play around with; we must not tempt God. We must not deny its danger, or begin to rationalize, as we are so prone to do. Rather we must turn to the sustaining Word of God and giving ourselves in homage to him acknowledge in the very fabric of our being that he is the Lord our God, and he alone do we serve, not our own desires. We take up our daily cross, for we have the privilege of being his disciples. Like him we are tempted so that like him we may, through a dying to self, come to the freedom of the risen life.

A Gift of Peace

"Peace—Peace be with you!" The Eleven certainly needed to hear these words, spoken with an authority that was creative. Fear, shame, remorse, despair, incredulous joy, struggling hope—all the emotions that surge through the being of the sinner in the process of conversion churned within the Lord's Apostles as he stood there before them. He fully understood their failure; he had foretold it, he took it upon himself, he had already fully healed it. All that was needed now was for them to accept—to accept the gift of his peace, the first gift of the Risen Lord, the ultimate gift that would bring all into harmony and communion.

The Lord's ministry of peace was not to end there, in that upper room. As he breathed upon them and poured out his healing and empowering Spirit—who from within would heal and begin a reign of comforting peace—he added: "Receive the Holy Spirit. Whose sins you shall forgive, they are forgiven them . . ." He had told them at the Supper less than seventy-two hours before: "The things you have seen me do, you will do, and greater than these." Now as he restored peace to their troubled and humbled spirits, he gave them the mission and power to be themselves ministers of pardon and peace.

Our Risen Lord's words can be heard by all of us. Each of us can be a minister of pardon and bring peace to the lives of others through forgiveness, loosening their burdens by our words of compassion and remission. Yet the Lord knows well those whom he has made, and all their needs. He knew the sinner's need to hear an authoritative word of pardon from the God he has abandoned and betrayed, and so he constituted a ministry of peace; he empowered his apostles and their successors to speak the word of peace authoritatively in his name.

Only gradually did the Church come to understand the fullness and the gratuity of the gifts she had received from her Lord and Founder. The early Church—as early as we have witness of—hoarded this precious gift. This powerful word of healing peace was authoritatively spoken only in the case of those sins which most blatantly violated peace: murder, apostasy, and the like. And one could hear the word addressed to oneself only once in a lifetime. After that, if one repeated a crime, one was left to the mercy of God without the comfort of the ministerial word. In time, the faith community came to understand more deeply the bounteous compassion of the Redeemer. The healing word was spoken over any grave sin and sinners could have recourse to it, if need be, again and again, as often as they were truly repentant.

For lesser sins, there was then, as now, other rites of healing. People could take holy water and, signing themselves with the saving cross, renew the grace of adoption. The Lord's prayer, "forgive us as we forgive," brought the

Father's forgiveness. The penitential rite at the beginning
of the communal celebration called down a general absolution. The monks who went out into the desert or into the
mountains, apart from the ecclesial community and its sac-
raments, sought the healing words of the *pneumaticos*, the
spiritual father. Those who sought purity of heart and
sinlessness went each night to this father to manifest the
thoughts of their hearts. Through the early centuries spiritual fathers were most frequently lay monks not endowed
with the powers of holy orders. They spoke a word of pardon and peace that had its authority from their own charis-
matic holiness. It was in Ireland, where the whole Church
was centered on the monasteries and the monks were the
priests and bishops, that the spiritual fathers, in response
to a manifestation of thoughts, frequently and even daily
spoke the authoritative sacramental word of pardon even
in response to minor stumblings. Their disciples were seeking absolute purity of heart. They wanted to be completely
reconciled with God, neighbor, and self. They wanted
repeated infusions of the sacramental grace of pardon to
reach down to the depths of their being, where the seven
capital sins were firmly rooted. As the great monastic missionaries went forth from Ireland to all parts of Chris-
tendom they carried with them the penitential books and
practices of their Church. Frequent confession even of
lesser sins and imperfections became the heritage of the
devout faithful everywhere.

Today there is in part a return to the earlier practice.
The sacrament of reconciliation seems to be more and
more reserved to the healing of more serious sins and more
is made of the other penitential rites of the liturgy to heal

us of our lesser sins and sinful inclinations. Yet the Church continues to ask that those who have cut themselves off through more serious sin be reconciled by the sacrament of the Church before entering again into communion. This is a recognition not only of the need of the power and authority of the Church in such reconciliation, but also of the need of paternal counsel and prayer. Since the time of the Irish missionaries it has been expected that the sacrament will ordinarily be ministered in a personal encounter with a spiritual father. The renewal of this sacrament after the Second Vatican Council has had this as its thrust. Even where there is a communal celebration of the sacrament, it is expected that each penitent will personally approach a priest for the confession of sins and absolution, thus providing the opportunity for personal response and counseling.

Among the early Cistercians, monks were expected to confess to the abbot, the spiritual father of the community. The abbot or his replacement often found himself hearing confessions in the course of the daily manual labor or at almost any other moment of the day. As monastic communities grew, there was necessarily a retreat from this demanding practice of daily manifestation of thoughts to the spiritual father, to the current practice of weekly confession, though more frequent confession is still found among the devout, especially where there are many spiritual fathers within a community.

The first Easter gift of the Risen Lord is a precious one. Wisdom as well as gratitude postulates our making good use of it. The renewal flowing from the Second Vatican Council has led us to call it now the Sacrament of Reconciliation. Most of the time we do not, by God's merciful care, need to be reconciled to God and his Church. The bond has not been ruptured by grave sin. But complete reconciliation with ourselves and our fellows is a lifetime work. The lesser faults and failures we bring to the sacrament direct its healing grace to their source, the sinful tendencies that are so deeply rooted in us, those basic tendencies we call the capital sins: pride, coveting, lust, anger, gluttony, envy, and sloth. Complete reconciliation will only be achieved when these tendencies have been eradicated and we are fully healed. This is one of the values of frequent confession. Sacramental confession not only means confronting our sinful tendencies and repenting our failures—we can do this each evening in our examen, and more frequently if we wish—it means bringing the restorative power of a specifically healing grace to our areas of need.

For many of us the reception of the sacrament of reconciliation is linked up with a meeting with our spiritual father. This is good. After laying bare our soul and exploring our progress and our failures, it is good if the spiritual father can direct sacramental healing to our wounds and weaknesses. But such a link is not always possible. Finding a good spiritual father—and a good one for us is one to whom we can confidently open our hearts, knowing he has the compassion and knowledge to help—is not always easy. We may have to travel a bit to find one. Or a good spiritual father may move away, or we may relocate at a distance from him so that we can meet only rarely or communicate by mail or phone. Or perhaps our guide is a lay person, man or woman. In this we would be returning to an earlier tradition. In such cases, should our celebration of the sacrament of reconciliation become infrequent, something we do only when necessary?

I don't think so. Even though we do have the sacramentals of reconciliation, such as I mentioned above (holy water, Mass rites, the Lord's Prayer, etc.) they are not a complete substitute for the powerful healing and peace-giving grace of the sacrament. Moreover, the Lord instituted the sacrament as a personal encounter. The present renewal has emphasized this. The priest is encouraged to add to a more intimate experience of sight and sound the sense of touch as he reaches out and lays his hand on the head of the penitent. But far more important, our broken-ness is spoken to by the compassion of a wounded healer who uses these human signs to communicate an attitude of heart that is sacramental of the Divine Compassion. Even if we do leave the manifestation of our deepest heart and our extended journey to our meetings with our spiritual father or mother, this human and divine sacramental encounter can be enlightening and strengthening, comforting and encouraging. It can keep us pressing forward on the path. It will heal us ever more deeply and integrally.

This is why monks frequently celebrate this sacrament. You may wonder how they can celebrate the sacrament when they have no sins to confess. What can they tell the priest? Our minor faults, our involuntary failings, our tendencies are enough when we relate them to the past sin out of which they flow and truly repent of these past failures. The grace of the sacrament will heal them in their root and lead us to an ever greater purity of heart. One who has been fully reconciled, who has true purity of heart, can be a greater channel of grace, can make Christ's reconciliation more available to others, to the world, can make Christ more present to this world. On the other hand, any lack of reconciliation draws off our energies, even if this lack lies hidden below the surface of our immediate consciousness. The grace of the sacrament reaches down into these unseen depths and accomplishes its healing work. Monthly confession would seem minimal for those taking their Christian growth seriously; weekly confession would not ordinarily be too much.

When our Risen Lord spoke his word of peace, he did not seek to establish merely some superficial contentment. He wanted to reestablish in the depths of our being the tranquillity that comes from the restoration of the order planned by God where the effects of sin are fully healed, the tendencies toward evil are redirected, and we are in complete harmony with ourselves, our fellows, and our God. The sacrament the Lord gifted his Church with on that day of Resurrection is a powerful gift to achieve this true peace which will be the source of constant peace in our own lives, in the lives of our families and communities, in the life of our society, our nation, and our world.

Blessed . . . Peacemakers

There was a great calm and peacefulness as the Patriarch
sat in his usual spot before the gate of the monastery—
quite different from yesterday. Then there were rumors,
followed by messengers with the fateful news: Totila, the
Goth, was on his way. The people from the surrounding
villages flocked up the mountain to consult their beloved
father. Not too many listened to his quiet, assuring words
of peace. Most had fled. And now the village and mountain was still, a land deserted. Abbot Benedict's own
monks moved about quietly in the depths of the great
abbey, their actions filled with a more intent prayer. The
hour was perilous indeed, and heaven was to be implored.
But, by and large, the monks shared the quiet faith and
peace that flowed from their father.

Then rumbling could be heard, first in the distance but
rapidly coming closer. A dust cloud rose above the dry road
from the north. It was a while before precise figures
emerged. The horde came rushing onward, lured by the
fabled wealth of the great abbey on the hilltop. Soon they
were ascending the steep mountain road. The Father sat

there serenely, as he did each day after lunch, to receive the petitions of the people. The somewhat less confident brothers gathered in the inmost depths of the immense building, huddled together in fervent prayer. Their loving support was with him.

In the end the feared Goth, awed by the sanctity of the monk, fell prostrate in his presence. It would be wonderful to know the thoughts, feelings, and emotions that raced through him in this moment of encounter. All history tells us is that when he remounted he went away in peace and was from that time on far less cruel.

When Louis VII of France and Geoffrey Plantagenet sat confronting each other in the large striped tent in the fields outside of Paris, the prospects for peace seemed very dim. The armies were arrayed, the knights spoiling for a fight. The rulers were animated with ambition and pride. The tent flap opened and a diminutive man in a long gray robe entered. In a moment the king of France was prostrate, the pretender of England on his knees. It was Bernard, the abbot of Clairvaux. When the monk left the tent, the lords knew they were brothers, a pact had been drawn and signed; the English pretender returned to his home in peace.

Monks have always been ministers of peace from the days of the great Antony, who emerged from the desert, through the days of Peter of Tarentaise, who stood before the Barbarossa, right up to our own times. In all the turmoil of Vietnam the Buddhist monks consistently stood for peace. And when a certain peace came to their own land they set out on a World Peace March to call all to that level of consciousness which can lead a nuclear society to true and lasting peace.

The call of the Christian to be a peacemaker is clear and unequivocal. We are called to follow Christ, to be his disciples. And he is the Prince of Peace. He is the Son of God and it is the peacemakers who will be called the sons of God. The danger is that we Christians in our peacemaking efforts will be drawn to interact at a secular or materialistic level, working only at economics and politics, and not make the unique contribution we can as persons of faith, empowered in oneness with Christ, creating the context for true and lasting peace. Saint Peter warns us: "Be on your guard lest you be led astray by the error of the wicked, and forfeit the security you enjoy."

Benedict and Bernard and the other true monastic peacemakers of history have been effective because they have acted from a deep source of peace within themselves, creating a context for peace. This is the contribution a Christian man or woman of peace can make. While the churches can and should mobilize their vast, well-organized structures for the peace effort and exert considerable economic and political influence, their most proper contribution will be at the level of the spirit. Men and women of the Church, along with those of other spiritual traditions, can and should bring a special contribution. Opening ourselves to allow the Spirit to create in us his fruit of peace, the peace that flows from love, we can become true sources of peace.

As Benedict and Bernard, monks and nuns are persons of peace because a certain asceticism frees them from the violence of their own passions. This does not mean that monks and nuns no longer have emotions, no longer experience love and anger, no longer are touched by the stirrings of ambition, vengefulness, lust. But a practiced asceticism teaches the monastic to recognize and accept these movements and then decide what to do with them: let them go while proceeding to what they really want to do; use them to energize a response to the situation; sublimate them into their opposite or other directions.

The monk and nun through the contemplative experience, which enables them to see themselves reflected in the eyes of God, know themselves. Only God can fully comprehend the beauty of the persons he has made, for he has made us in his image and likeness. When we come to know our own beauty, our value, our being in God, we are eminently free in the face of what others think and say, how they evaluate us. It is not that the monastics do not seek the support and appreciation of others. For this we enter into a community of love. We want it and we seek it for we are greatly helped by it—just like everyone else. But we are not dependent upon it. Therefore, it does not dictate our actions. We can say and do what we know we should with great peace, for we are not dependent upon the acceptance of others. We act out of the Source, the center where we are always coming forth from the infinite and all-affirming love of God.

Our *lectio*, our listening engenders in us a deep faith; faith comes from hearing. We know we have not here a lasting dwelling place, we are en route, we are pilgrims. With death, life is not ended but changed. And so, even in the face of death, we can be at peace, like Saint Benedict sitting at the gates of Monte Cassino. Death has lost its sting. We are free in the face of death because we have put our stock in the deeper, unending life of the spirit. This does not mean we do not value life. Knowing all life from its Source, we savor life far more fully than one who clings to it with anxiety. We know the sacredness of life, the quality it should have, and we seek to promote that. Visitors to most monasteries are struck by the beauty of the monastic domain, the good life the monks live, the warmth of the hospitality, the reverence shown to guests, the prevailing peace.

The experience of God, whom we constantly seek, the Source of all life, who has all things in his loving fatherly hands, leaves us secure and at peace, even in the face of nuclear holocaust. "He's got the whole wide world in his hand." God does have everything under control. His thoughts are not always our thoughts, nor our ways his ways. But in the end, his will will be done, on earth as in heaven.

There is a constant danger of our forgetting this, at least in practice, and acting and strategizing as though all depended upon us. In God's design much does depend on us. We have our responsibility—our ability to respond to his call and leadership and participate in the creation of a new heaven and earth. But we can be at peace if we remember results are his business. "One sows, another waters, God gives the increase." We can be profoundly at peace and create a context of peace for others, surrounding them with caring love and listening attentively to the communication of their hearts, if we ourselves are in touch with the Source of peace and are acting out of that Source.

We can do this by regularly making time to let everything else go and rest in the Source at the center of our being (which we can do through Centering Prayer or any other legitimate method of meditation). Making time and letting things go, even our own thoughts, feelings, and desires, is a real asceticism that sets us free and leaves us at peace. The experience of God and of our own beauty in God enables us to act with great freedom and love. We can create the space within which others can discover their own beauty and power. They can let go of their defensiveness and get in touch with their true aspirations, realizing the oneness of the basic aspirations shared by all fellow travelers on this globe. The contemplative experience of God, Creator of All, understood through the teaching of our Master, the Prince of Peace, is the powerful and unique contribution that we can bring to a threatened world. Universal caring and sharing, because we are all one in our Source, will lead to a world where there will be no one to fight, no one to arm against, none of the injustices that cry out for vengeance. In a word, they will lead to a new level of consciousness.

We desperately need this new level of consciousness. Never has it been known in the history of men and nations, that a people have stockpiled weapons and have not used them. But if we use our stockpiles we will not be here long enough to know it—nor will anyone else. We have to break with this pattern of the past and create a new pattern. We have to be free enough to destroy our own weapons, free enough to go beyond where we are and find a new mode of security in a prevailing climate of oneness and trust, of human solidarity. Is there really any hope we can do this as a global people?

Prayer can be effective of this through its intercessory power, harnessing the creative energy which is presently bringing forth the hearts of us all. The same God who hardened the heart of Pharaoh can soften the hearts of today's leaders, and of all of us. He can form in us new hearts. When God creates he does not abandon his creation; he doesn't make something, set it on its own feet, and walk away, as might a human carpenter. What he makes exists because at each moment he shares with it something of his own unique being. If he turned his attention from it, it would cease to exist. God is constantly bringing forth all that is. And he has willed that the way he brings it forth is in part determined by us: "Ask, and it shall be done for you." This is the intercessory power of our prayer. It can bring about a global transformation through the divine, ever-active, creative power of our God.

Prayer can also be effective through the transformation of consciousness it effects in us the pray-ers (we cannot constantly pray for peace and meditate on peace and not become more profoundly men and women of peace) and through us the rest of our species. Ken Keyes in a fascinating and powerful little book, *The Hundredth Monkey*, recounts an incident which took place in Japan in the 1950s:

> In 1952, on the island of Koshima, scientists were providing monkeys with sweet potatoes dropped in the sand. The monkeys liked the taste of the raw sweet potatoes, but they found the dirt unpleasant.
>
> An 18-month old female named Imo found she could solve the problem by washing the potatoes in a

nearby stream. She taught the trick to her mother. Her playmates also learned the new way and they taught their mothers too.

This cultural innovation was gradually picked up by various monkeys before the eyes of the scientists. Between 1952 and 1958, all the young monkeys learned to wash the sandy sweet potatoes to make them more palatable.

Only the adults who imitated their children learned this social improvement. Other adults kept eating the dirty sweet potatoes. Then something startling took place. In the autumn of 1958, a certain number of Koshima monkeys were washing sweet potatoes—the exact number is not known. Let us suppose that when the sun rose one morning there were 99 monkeys on Koshima Island who had learned to wash their sweet potatoes. Let's further suppose that later that morning the hundredth monkey learned to wash potatoes. *Then it happened!*

By that evening almost everyone in the tribe was washing sweet potatoes before eating them. The added energy of the hundredth monkey somehow created an ideological breakthrough! But notice. The most surprising thing observed by these scientists was that the habit of washing sweet potatoes then spontaneously jumped over the sea—Colonies of monkeys on other islands and the mainland troop monkeys at Takasakiyama began washing their sweet potatoes.

Keyes postulates that "when a certain critical number achieves an awareness, this new awareness may be com-

municated from mind to mind . . . there is a point at
which if only one more person tunes in to a new awareness
a field is strengthened so that this awareness reaches almost everyone!"

The idea that the consciousness of one person can affect
that of others is not new; that the transformation of consciousness of some can affect the whole. This is found expressed in many traditions. It is the leaven of the Gospel
parable that leavens the whole. It is the attainment of
Teilhard de Chardin's noosphere. It is not primarily quan-
tity that makes the difference, it is quality. In prayer, in
meditation, we take on more and more the mind of Christ,
the Prince of Peace, the peacemaker par excellence. "For
in him is our peace." We see the awesomeness of all life.
The reverence that is the basis of a true ecology, of just
stewardship, comes to possess us. Through prayer, our consciousness is transformed and because of the intimate in-
terconnection of all human persons we become instrumen-
tal in that transformation of consciousness that will set the
human family on another course of action. Prayer will put
us into intimate contact with the Source of all peace. It
will establish peace in us. We will act out of the center of
peace. We will have an invincible hope because it will be
grounded on an unconquerable faith. The kind of faith out
of which Saint Peter wrote to us, as I have quoted in the
Introduction: "We await *a new* heaven and *a new* earth
where, according to his promise, the justice of God will
reside."

Even in the face of an apparently total catastrophe there
is still cause for hope. Christ was destroyed on the cross
and rose again. A new earth and God's full justice is to

come to us. If we are tempted to lose patience with the apparently ceaseless and senseless arms race, "consider that our Lord's patience is directed toward salvation." Rather than being "led astray by the error of the wicked," by the idolatry that puts its hope in arms, we need to grow "in the knowledge of our Lord and Savior Jesus Christ" so that we can see that he is working in and through all. We do this through prayer.

I do not emphasize prayer here to downplay the importance of other activities and efforts for disarmament and the pursuit of universal peace in justice and love. God does work in and through the activities and efforts of men and women. But we cannot sustain such activities and efforts if we do not have hope. Prayer renews our faith and lets us powerfully experience that we do have cause for hope.

When we have convictions in regard to the power of a life that is centered to create peace we can then, as peacemakers, seek to open this dimension of peace to others. We can share this aspect of the Christian tradition by teaching Centering Prayer or other forms of Christian meditation, forming meditation groups, introducing periods of meditative prayer into our meetings and rallies. If we act out of this source, then our activities will be peaceful, creating a context for peace, and not engender any of the hostility or perpetuate any of the violence from which we seek to free ourselves and our global family.

Act we must. True love and concern postulate it. And there are many forms our activity can take besides propagating a contemplative approach to life which sources true peace. Recently the president of a multinational wrote with great frankness: "They (the Soviets) wouldn't even have been in the arms race had it not been for the incredible volume of loans made directly to the Soviet Union by U.S. banks . . . we continue to throw good money after bad . . ." Besides praying for those who make the decisions in the great banking and trading corporations that they may use their power more creatively for peace, we can hold minimal stock in such corporations and animate stockholders' interest to monitor and direct their activity. We can effectively support boycotts. We can use the media to protest the activities of war and support those of peace. We can seek direct communication with persons whose ideology or nationality is labeled "the enemy."

This does not seem to me to be the place to catalog a long list of things to do or that can be done. As a spiritual community, a community inspirited by the Spirit of Christ, we can make our essential contribution of creating a context for peace. Then we can count on the same Holy Spirit to guide us in concrete activities in our own lives and in the life of our communities. We can seek peace and pursue it. Realizing we are each presently at different places, each with our own unique role, we can all pledge ourselves to depth, to openness, to readiness, to take the next step in faithfulness, to be blessed peacemakers, true sons and daughters of our God of Peace.

Postword

I have been sharing a number of values and disciplines which belong to our Christian tradition going back to the earliest times. It is true that today and in many ages they have been perhaps most consciously and evidentially lived out in the lives of monks and nuns. But they belong to the common heritage of *all* Christians, grounded as they are on the teaching of our Lord, Jesus, and lived by the first Jerusalem community. I have written of them in the monastic context because that is the context within which I have best come to know them and live them. It is in this context that men and women have approached me asking for this sharing. I have dared to suggest a few concrete ways these values and practices could possibly be incorporated into lay life. These suggestions come largely from the lived experiences of friends such as Commander Moran. I am hesitant to dictate or even suggest such ways on my own. Once they have become acquainted with these values and practices, with a little courageous experimentation all persons will with the help of the Holy Spirit quickly get a sense of how they can incorporate them into their lives and the life of their household or community.

There are two things which stand out for me at this moment as being especially important. The first is the wholeness of our vision as Christians. It might be expressed as "having the mind of Christ." But this needs elaboration. I fear too many in the name of spirituality fail to appreciate and incorporate adequately into their perspective and into their living experience certain aspects of themselves as human being and certain aspects of God's good creation. I know there was a time when I did. There is no gulf between God and his creation, between the sacred and the secular; there is a continuum. I even hesitate to say there is a lower and higher. There is rather a varied participation in and expression of the divine goodness and beauty. Every person, everything in creation is sacred; it has something of the divine. Every action is energized by God no matter how much it may be diverted by our malice. More important—there is no human person who is not truly the image of God no matter how overlaid that person may be with human misery and malice. We do not lose our likeness to our Father even when we restrict the sunshine of our love and the rain of our compassion to the good, or even if we save them for the evil! The realization of this omnipresence of goodness and beauty, of him whom I love, has made life a very beautiful and rich thing for me. Many have asked me if I were not horrified by the poverty and disease I saw in India. If one looks at India (and many other places) from a material point of view, it is misery beyond toleration. But if one looks at India with a holistic perception, it is a tremendously beautiful people in all its richness. As a more integral vision grew in me over the years, the residue of earlier prejudices against Blacks and Jews and non-Catholics slipped away, and later-induced prejudices against gays, activists, and communists were invalidated. I enjoy the beauty of all persons now; I touch the goodness in them. We may see things very differently, but at root we are all children of one Father. We all share one humanity, we sincerely seek what seems good to us and struggle with our human frailty. I enjoy the beauty of each created thing. Possessing nothing, I possess all. Things often belong more fully to me than to their supposed owner—I get more out of them. The best things in life are free.

At the same time, my life is big enough not only to hold in some way in this context of goodness all the world's pain and misery, but to be able to do something about it. The quality of my life, its love, making present his love, can and does raise it all. In this I rejoice. A holistic view is broad, expansive, deep, rich—very rich and full. It is the only view worthy of a human, of a Christian, a true child of God, an empowered co-redeemer with Christ.

It is important to have such a view; it may take time to develop it. It is important to live out of such a view; and this is the exciting and challenging task of our lives. Herein comes the second point that seems eminently important to me. It will never be enough just to *wish* we could see things this way or live like Christ, as a disciple of Christ. We have to be eminently practical about such wishes and make them efficacious desires by practical planning and action. Otherwise, wishes will remain wishes when life is regretfully ended.

Let me suggest a few thoughts in regard to practical action. I think a practical course of action should include assessment, planning, implementation, and evaluation.

Confronted by a value, we need to make as assessment: Is it a value for me? Is it implemented in my life? How? Could it be more fully appreciated and lived? How? What models and supports can I draw on? How does it fit in with the other values in my life? How will it fit in with the values and the lives of those with whom I most intimately share my life?

Once all the data are in, I come to planning: What needs to be done? How am I going to do it? How am I going to get the support I need to do it?

Then comes the doing. There is no substitute for actual performance, whether it be the interior action of actual acceptance or the exterior concrete act.

Finally, there is evaluation—a periodical checkup on my performance. When a young man enters a traditional Byzantine monastery he is asked to appear before his spiritual father each evening to manifest his thoughts. This daily regime of accountability is very demanding. The novice makes rapid progress toward purity of heart. For most of us a much less exacting regime is necessary and to be recommended. A weekly or monthly review of our plan and its implementation, and an updating of our assessment will be adequate to help us move along and give us a deep sense of satisfaction in our lives. This evaluation is much enhanced when it can be done with another or others, especially if this involves our support network. A journey together is always more exciting and much easier and more secure. "A brother who helps a brother is like a walled city." Set up a date to meet regularly with someone who can support you. Don't complete any meeting with that person without confirming the next date. If an appointment is missed, set another one up immediately. Keep someone in your life who will keep you honest and keep you moving.

There is so much more I can say about evaluation. And certainly about the other three points: assessment, planning, and implementation. But I do not want to write another book. Your own practice will soon fill out all I have written. Go ahead and do it!